TAX POLICIES IN THE 1979 BUDGET

HIGHLIGHTS OF A CONFERENCE

Washington, D.C.
February 27, 1978

Edited by Rudolph G. Penner

American Enterprise Institute for Public Policy Research
Washington, D.C.

Rudolph G. Penner is director of Tax Policy Studies at the American Enterprise Institute. The assistance of Emily Bardeen is gratefully acknowledged.

Price $2.75 per copy

ISBN 0-8447-1329-5

Library of Congress Catalog Card No. 78–58911

Printed in the United States of America

PARTICIPANTS

Ahmad Al-Samarrie, Office of Management and Budget

Martin Bailey, Department of Economics, University of Maryland

J. Gregory Ballentine, Department of Economics, Wayne State University

John Barnum, American Enterprise Institute

William Baroody, Jr., American Enterprise Institute

Bruce Bartlett, Office of Congressman Kemp

John Berry, Forbes

Michael J. Boskin, Department of Economics, Stanford University

Charles Bradford, Joint Economic Committee

David F. Bradford, Department of Economics and Public Affairs, Woodrow Wilson School, Princeton University

Ralph Bristol, U.S. Department of the Treasury

James M. Buchanan, Jr., Center for the Study of Public Choice, Virginia Polytechnic Institute and State University

Bruce Davie, Office of Management and Budget

Martha Davis, U.S. Department of Commerce

David Einhorn, U.S. Department of Housing and Urban Development

William Fellner, American Enterprise Institute

Bill Frenzel, U.S. House of Representatives

George M. von Furstenberg, Department of Economics, Indiana University

Harvey Galper, U.S. Department of the Treasury

Carl Gasperow, Coopers and Lybrand

David Gergen, American Enterprise Institute

Jerry Green, Department of Economics, Harvard University

Gottfried Haberler, American Enterprise Institute

Daniel Halperin, U.S. Department of the Treasury

John Hamm, Office of Senator John D. Danforth

Arthur Hauptman, House Budget Committee

Robert Helms, American Enterprise Institute

Harold Hochman, City University of New York

Ronald Hoffman, U.S. Department of the Treasury

Darwin Johnson, Office of Management and Budget

Thomas Johnson, American Enterprise Institute

Martin Katz, Office of Senator Daniel P. Moynihan

W. Thomas Kelly, C.L.U., CEO, First Investment Annuity Company of America

Robert Kilpatrick, Office of Management and Budget

William Lilley III, House Budget Committee

Nelson McClung, U.S. Department of the Treasury

Charles E. McLure, Jr., Rice University and National Bureau of Economic Research

Sid Moore, American Enterprise Institute

Lynn Murphy, Taxation with Representation

Peggy Musgrave, University of California at Berkeley

Richard A. Musgrave, Department of Economics, Harvard University

John S. Nolan, Miller and Chevalier

Ben Okner, U.S. Department of the Treasury

Van Dorn Ooms, Senate Budget Committee

Attiat Ott, Department of Economics, Clark University

William C. Penick, Arthur Anderson & Co.

Rudolph G. Penner, American Enterprise Institute

Howard Penniman, American Enterprise Institute

George L. Perry, The Brookings Institution

Austin Ranney, American Enterprise Institute

Mark Ratner, U.S. House of Representatives

Craig Roberts, Office of Senator Orrin G. Hatch

Alan Rothenberg, Ways and Means Committee

Bernard Saffran, Department of Economics, Swarthmore College

Jerry Shipley, Office of Management and Budget

Laurence Silberman, American Enterprise Institute

William Springer, Council of Economic Advisers

Emil M. Sunley, U.S. Department of the Treasury

Eric Toder, U.S. Department of the Treasury

Norman Ture, Norman Ture, Inc.

Allen Unsworth, House Budget Committee

Beatrice Vaccara, U.S. Department of the Treasury

Robert Vogel, Department of Economics, Southern Illinois University at Carbondale

Jude Wanniski, The Wall Street Journal

John Weicher, The Urban Institute

James Wetzler, Joint Committee on Taxation

John Wilkins, U.S. Department of the Treasury

CONTENTS

PREFACE

On January 20, 1978, President Carter presented the Congress with a long list of recommended tax cuts and tax reforms. Although the recommended tax reforms are somewhat less radical than had been expected earlier, they are still significant and have therefore become highly controversial.

The American Enterprise Institute for Public Policy Research sponsored a conference on *Tax Policies in the 1979 Budget* on February 27, 1978. The conference brought together experts on tax policy from the academic world, government, business, and the press to exchange their views and to enhance the public discussion of tax policy issues. This booklet reproduces the six papers delivered to the conference and briefly summarizes the discussion that followed.

PART ONE

MACROECONOMIC ASPECTS

Tax Cuts and the Economic Outlook

George L. Perry

The administration has proposed a permanent tax cut amounting to $25 billion at 1979 levels of income. Most of the cut is to be effective at the start of FY1979, with individual income taxes reduced by $18 billion, corporate taxes by $5 billion, and excise and unemployment insurance taxes by $2 billion. The individual and corporate reductions are the net balance between tax cuts and revenue-raising reforms. While other papers in this conference will discuss the proposed reductions and reforms in some detail, I will deal with them in as aggregated a form as consideration of the economic outlook allows.

So as not to get bogged down in disagreements about what objectives economic policy should pursue, I will accept the broad goals of the administration: First, a 4.5 to 5 percent annual growth rate of real GNP is expected for 1978 and 1979 by the Council of Economic Advisers, so I assume they want real growth at least that fast. Second, the present rate of inflation should be reduced and should eventually level off at a rate that is acceptable. In the first two parts of this paper I shall examine the tax cut in the context of the real growth objectives in the short and long run. In the last part, I will raise some issues about the objective of curbing inflation.

The Tax Cut and Aggregate Demand

The tax cut is only one element of a general fiscal policy affecting the economic outlook. And fiscal policy, in turn, is only one of the major stabilization instruments affecting aggregate demand, monetary policy being the other. In order to focus on the tax cuts, expenditures can be projected from known budget proposals and recent experience. And I will assume monetary policy is accommodative to the extent that short-term interest rates rise gradually, if at all, with a real GNP growth rate of 4 percent, and rise no more than 100 basis points in a year of 5 percent real growth. On past experience, this pattern is roughly consistent with meeting or slightly exceeding the recent targets for the monetary aggregate set by the Federal Reserve.

The High-Employment Surplus. The proposed tax cut is part of an overall fiscal policy that is less expansionary than some frequently cited budget figures suggest.

I am grateful to Jesse Abraham and Judith Colle for their help in the presentation of this paper. The views in this paper are my own and not necessarily those of the officers or trustees of The Brookings Institution.

1

It is by now widely recognized that the back-to-back $60 billion deficits expected for FY1978 and FY1979 are enlarged by the operation of automatic stabilizers and do not provide a useful measure of the budget's impact on the economy. Even the analysis of the high-employment surplus that is shown in this year's budget [1]

TABLE 1

HIGH-EMPLOYMENT SURPLUS ESTIMATES, FY1977–FY1979

(billions of dollars)

Estimates of *High-Employment Surplus*	*FY1977*	*FY1978*	*FY1979*
1. Office of Management and Budget (unified budget)	−10	−32	−37
2. Adjusted to national income and product accounts	−13	−25	−28
3. Adjusted for spending overestimates	−13	−18	−24

SOURCE: Unified budget estimates from *The Budget of the United States Government, Fiscal Year 1979*, p. 41. The other estimates were made by the author.

overstates the fiscal stimulus that is occurring. This surplus, shown in the top line of Table 1, is the difference between estimated outlays and receipts at high employment on the basis of a unified budget.[2] By this measure, the high-employment deficit grows by $27 billion between FY1977 and FY1979 when the tax cut takes full effect.

Two adjustments are made to these deficit estimates in lines 2 and 3 of the table. In line 2, the Office of Management and Budget (OMB) deficits of line 1 are converted to be consistent with national income and product accounts (NIPA). The NIPA budget concept excludes purely financial transactions and adjusts the timing of most receipts to when the liabilities are incurred. It is recognized as the budget concept that best characterizes the impact on the economy of the budget's fiscal policy. Because the difference between the unified and NIPA budgets changes considerably after FY1977, both the size of the deficits and, even more markedly, the growth in the deficits are smaller on the basis of NIPA.

In line 3 the NIPA deficits are adjusted for likely shortfalls in expenditures below present projections. Actual spending has fallen substantially below the original budget projections in five of the last six years. In FY1977 the shortfall was $13.7 billion, the biggest one yet. Currently, the Congressional Budget Office expects spending for FY1978 will be at least $7 billion below the present OMB estimate of $462 billion (unified budget basis).[3] In line 3 the FY1978 high-employment deficit is reduced by this $7 billion. The FY1979 deficit is reduced by $4 billion. This last is a guess, based on the fact that OMB is trying to bring estimates and outlays closer together, but so far without success.

The estimates of line 3 show fiscal policy is growing only moderately more expansionary this fiscal year (1978) and next. The increase in the high-employment deficit is only about 0.25 percent of GNP in each year. Larger changes than this have occurred in five of the seven years since 1970. With an accommodating monetary policy, changes of this size would be expected to add roughly 0.5 percent to real output.

2

The FY1979 deficit in line 3 is, coincidentally, just about equal to the size of the proposed tax cut. Given the expected level of expenditures, the high-employment NIPA budget would nearly balance without the tax cut in FY1979. In this case, fiscal policy would make a restrictive swing of about 0.75 percent of GNP.[4]

The quarterly or half-yearly path of the high-employment budget would show a more erratic pattern but would tell a qualitatively similar story. In the second half of calendar year 1977, the high-employment deficit jumped by $25 billion to a level of $30 billion. This abrupt change came primarily as a consequence of sharp increases from the first half of the year in grants to state and local governments ($9.5 billion), purchases ($11 billion), and transfers ($5.5 billion). The economic impact of this fiscal stimulus will be felt for several more quarters. But fiscal policy itself will be generally more restrictive, with falling high-employment deficits until the last quarter of 1978, when the bulk of the tax cut is effective, and falling deficits again in subsequent quarters. Without allowing for spending shortfalls, the Council of Economic Advisers estimates *calendar* year high-employment deficits of −$18 billion, −$27 billion, and −$23 billion for 1977, 1978, and 1979 respectively.[5]

The Composition of the Tax Cut. The high-employment surplus provides only an approximation of the budget's impact on aggregate economic activity. A given dollar change in the surplus will have a somewhat different impact depending on whether it comes from a change in purchases, transfers, or grants or from any of the many ways in which tax revenues can be changed. The proposed tax cut reduces personal income taxes, some minor excise taxes, and the corporate tax rate; it strengthens and extends the investment tax credit and raises taxes on some business activities. In consideration of the economic outlook, I want to focus on the division between tax cuts for business and for individuals.

The proposed personal tax cuts can be expected to affect consumer spending in the usual way. Little tax reform has been proposed and the cuts are permanent so there is none of the uncertainty that may surround the impact of temporary tax changes or tax rebates on spending. I would expect at least 90 percent of the aggregate tax reduction to show up as higher consumer spending. Part of the spending effect should be immediate, and virtually all of the first round should be felt by late 1979. If anything, one might argue for a spending impact that was somewhat larger and prompter than average because the current consumer saving rate is low and because real taxes have been rising as a consequence of both inflation and increases in payroll taxes. Within reasonable limits, if the distribution of the net tax cuts were altered from that proposed by the administration, the response in total consumption would not be significantly changed. Differences in marginal spending propensities at different income levels are not important enough to alter the expected spending response in the aggregate.

There is little professional consensus on the size and timing of the spending response to be expected from changes in business taxes. A recent study by the Congressional Budget Office (CBO), using three large econometric models to analyze the response to three alternative tax changes, illustrates the range of uncertainty on this question.[6] In the third year after enactment of the tax change, business fixed investment would be greater by between 55 and 255 percent of the annual revenue loss from enlarging the investment credit on equipment. Investment would be greater by between 50 and 86 percent of the annual revenue loss from reducing the corporate profits tax. In both cases, the investment per dollar of revenue loss in the first year would be only from 10 to 15 percent as great as these third-year effects. The study also notes that accelerated depreciation would initially generate substantial investment per dollar of revenue loss simply because the revenue loss would occur over a period after an investment is made. In its third year, a 20 percent reduction in the tax life for plant and equipment would cost about $3 billion in revenue. This change would have an impact on investment spending similar to that of an enlargement of investment credit costing $3 billion a year in revenues.

Uncertain as it is, this evidence does suggest that corporate tax reduction stimulates total spending less than personal tax cuts do and that it very probably stimulates investment spending less than enlargements of investment credit or faster depreciation write-offs do. If corporate rate reduction could have an especially favorable effect on stock prices, and if that in turn could have a favorable effect on investment spending, corporate rate reduction would look better as an investment stimulus than these conclusions from the econometric models suggest.

For the near-term economic outlook, the composition of the tax cuts suggests fiscal policy may have a somewhat smaller expansionary effect than the high-employment budget analysis suggests. The $6 billion of business tax cuts just equals the increase in the high-employment deficit for FY1979. If spending from such cuts is very slow in coming, fiscal policy as a whole may not be expansionary at all between FY1978 and FY1979.

TABLE 2

FORECASTS OF REAL GNP
(percent changes)

Source [a]	1977–1978 [b]	1978–1979 [b]
Conference Board	4.2	5.1
Congressional Budget Office	4.3	4.1
Council of Economic Advisers	4.75	4.75
Data Resources Institute	4.0	4.0 [c]
Wharton	4.8	3.1

[a] When a range is given by the source, the midpoint of the range is shown in the table.
[b] The period is from the fourth quarter of one year to the fourth quarter of the next.
[c] Forecast is for calendar year 1978 to calendar year 1979.

The Economic Outlook. The economy entered 1978 with some momentum. A sample of forecasts for real GNP growth from inside and outside the government is presented in Table 2. The expected growth rates range from 4.0 to 4.8 percent between the fourth quarter of 1977 and the fourth quarter of 1978. All projections include the proposed tax cut except for that of the Conference Board which assumes a slightly smaller cut. Although the coal strike will shift some activity from the first to the second quarter, a 4 percent average rate of expansion until the tax cut

4

takes effect seems a reasonable forecast. By the end of the year, the tax cut will probably be needed to keep the expansion from running out of gas. And it could be needed sooner. There is still no evidence of a strong pickup in business investment, and stronger demands from abroad are more a wish than a reality. It is doubtful that housing starts will rise further. And the consumer saving rate was already on the low side in the second half of 1977.

In this environment, there is no justification for a sharp rise in interest rates. There would be much to gain and little at risk in moving up the effective date of the tax cuts, but since a new budget resolution would be required an earlier cut is unlikely.

In 1979, after the initial stimulus from the tax cut, fiscal policy will be turning more restrictive. Continued economic expansion at a rate that continues to reduce unemployment will depend on growing strength from outside the federal sector. The forecasts of real GNP growth in Table 2 for the interval from fourth quarter 1978 to fourth quarter 1979 range from 3.1 to 5.1 percent. Only the Conference Board anticipates more growth than in the preceding four quarters. It also forecasts 5.6 percent unemployment by the end of 1979, the lowest unemployment rate projected.

The Tax Cut and the Longer Run

In the outlook beyond the immediate future, the proposed tax cut can be viewed as part of fiscal policy for subsequent years. For this longer run, it is useful to ask what high-employment surplus policy should aim for and whether the tax cut is consistent with achieving the desired surplus. There is clearly no single answer to either of these questions. But an analysis based on expenditure plans already outlined by the administration offers some guidance, and the strength of demands outside the federal sector provide additional evidence.

In line 1 of Table 3 the administration's budget projections are shown through FY1982. They exceed projections of a "current services" budget to the extent that they include new or expanded programs already planned for and, to a lesser extent, reflect planned reductions on some current programs.

In line 2 these projections are adjusted to bring expenditures for FY1981–1982 up to 21 percent of GNP, an announced goal of the President. For FY1981 the adjustment allows expenditures of only $11 billion more than present budget projections, but by FY1982 there is room for $29 billion more. The 21 percent goal does not seem unrealistic.

The high-employment surplus adjustments in lines 3 through 6 correspond to those made in Table 1. Line 6 shows NIPA surpluses implicit in the OMB budget projections after adjusting them for near-term spending shortfalls and allowing for additional spending in FY1981–1982 to reach the 21 percent target.

The proposed tax cut leaves ample scope for achieving balance or surpluses in future high-employment budgets. But do the high-employment surpluses that emerge after FY1980 provide enough demand to achieve and maintain high employment? Or, alternatively, could even larger surpluses be required in order to avoid excess demand or a tight monetary policy that would inhibit investment spending? A sectoral analysis helps answer these questions. Table 4 shows sec-

TABLE 3

The Tax Cut and High-Employment Budget Projections
(billions of dollars)

	FY1977	FY1978	FY1979	FY1980	FY1981	FY1982
Unified budget expenditures						
1. Office of Management and Budget projections	397	459	498	541	574	612
2. Adjusted to 21 percent of GNP, 1981–1982	397	459	498	541	585	641
High-employment surplus						
3. Office of Management and Budget projections	−10	−32	−37	−19	16	42
4. Adjusted to national income and product accounts	−13	−25	−28	−11	24	50
5. Adjusted for spending shortfalls, 1978–1979	−13	−18	−24	−11	24	50
6. Adjusted to spending target of 21 percent of GNP, 1981–1982	−13	−18	−24	−11	13	21
7. Projections from line 6, without tax cut	−13	−16	0	12	37	49

Source: See Table 1.

toral balances of saving and investment (net surpluses) during previous periods of high employment and contrasts them with actual 1977 balances and 1977 balances projected at high employment. The sectoral breakdown is arranged to highlight the gross receipts of the business sector and its investment spending.

Other things being equal, an unusually large surplus (or small deficit) in any sector is a source of weak total demand and large deficits in the federal sector. The large actual surpluses shown for the foreign sector and state and local government thus help account for the large federal deficit today.[7] Together they amounted to 2.5 percent of GNP in 1977, compared with an average of slightly more than zero in the six high-employment years. Although some trend toward surpluses is evident in the successive high-employment periods, the total surplus of the foreign sector and state and local government in 1977 was one percentage point more than even the 1972–1973 average. Adjusted to high-employment levels, it is 1.7 percentage points higher. Of all the sectors, only the personal sector had an unusually small surplus in 1977, reflecting the relatively low fraction of disposable income that was saved.

The high-employment projections in the last three columns provide a basis for evaluating the fiscal policy that will be needed in the future. Although they are anchored to the actual 1977 economy, the high-employment projections can be thought of as applying to any year in the near future. Based on historical responses of incomes and demands to higher levels of GNP, projections are made directly for all receipts and expenditures in the table except one, which is calculated as a

6

TABLE 4

Sectoral Surpluses as a Percentage of GNP

Net Surplus	Previous High-Employment Periods				Actual 1977 (5)	1977 High Employment		
	1955–1956 (1)	1965–1966 (2)	1972–1973 (3)	Average (4)		Actual fiscal policy (6)	With tax cut (7)	Tax cut and optimistic demands (8)
Business								
Gross retained earnings	11.7	12.2	11.0	11.6	12.0	12.4	12.7	12.7
Fixed investment	−10.0	−10.6	−10.2	−10.3	−9.8	(−12.4)	(−11.6)	11.6
Inventory building	−1.3	−1.6	−1.1	−1.3	−0.9	−1.0	−1.0	−1.0
Net surplus	0.4	0	−0.3	0	1.3	(−1.0)	(0.1)	0.1
Residential construction	−5.8	−4.2	−5.2	−5.1	−4.8	−4.8	−4.8	−4.8
Personal	4.6	4.4	4.8	4.5	3.6	3.5	3.6	3.6
Foreign	0	−0.4	0.4	0	1.0	1.4	1.4	0.5 [a]
State and local government								
Trust funds	0.3	0.5	0.7	0.5	0.8	0.8	0.8	0.8
General funds	−0.6	−0.5	0.4	−0.2	0.7	1.0	1.0	0
Federal government	1.3	−0.1	−1.0	0.1	−2.6	−0.9	−2.1	(0)

[a] Reduces net exports of goods and services in the national income and product accounts to zero.

Note: The sum of sectoral net surpluses differs from zero by the statistical discrepancy. Figures in parentheses are calculated as the residuals from other sectoral entries.

residual from the others since the balance for all sectors must net to zero. In columns 6 and 7 the residual is the business sector (and business fixed investment). In column 8 it is the federal sector. An accommodating monetary policy is implicit in these projections. This is particularly important if residential construction outlays in the high-employment economy are to make up the same proportion of GNP as in 1977. Any substantial rise in interest rates would be expected to reduce the share of construction and probably even reduce the actual level of construction. In the projections, consumption is increased by 93 percent of increases in disposable income. In the projections of columns 6 and 7, both the foreign and state and local government surpluses are allowed to increase from actual levels. Imports and tax revenues rise with the higher level of GNP, while no offsetting increase in demand in these sectors is assumed. This assumption is altered in the projections of column 8.

The Business Sector. The gross retained earnings of the business sector were relatively high in 1977, having recovered from somewhat depressed levels earlier in the decade. This is particularly apparent in the high-employment projections of column 6. When the proposed business tax cuts are added in column 7, the high-employment projection of gross retained earnings reaches 12.7 percent of GNP, a full percentage point above the average of the six previous high-employment years and half a point above the previous high in 1965–1966.

As a consequence of these high ratios of gross retained earnings in the business sector together with relatively large surpluses elsewhere, high levels of business investment are needed to achieve high employment. In columns 6 and 7 the business fixed investment ratio and the business surplus ratio that are needed are shown in parentheses; they are calculated as the residuals from the other sectoral entries. With the actual 1978 budget, adjusted only by its automatic stabilizers (column 6), business fixed investment would have had to be an extraordinary 12.4 percent of GNP for high employment to be achieved. The proposed tax cut (column 7) enlarges the federal deficit and consumer demand, thus reducing the needed business investment at high employment to 11.6 percent of GNP. This is still a historically large percentage and represents spending 25 percent higher than actual 1977 levels. But it may lie within the optimistic bounds of a projection for the future.

Investment spending for energy conservation could be substantial in the near future, and this factor was not present in the earlier years used for comparison. Spending for pollution abatement will continue, and this factor was previously important only in 1972–1973. In addition, compared with the last two high-employment periods, but not with the mid-1950s, the price deflator for investment has risen relative to GNP. Thus a higher fraction of nominal GNP would be needed to achieve the same real investment fraction. The tax reductions themselves provide new incentives to investment, especially the extension of the 10 percent investment credit to structures. As noted earlier, gross retained earnings in column 7 are an unusually high percentage of GNP, which in itself may encourage investment spending. There are, however, negative elements in the investment outlook as well. The present inflation rate provides some disincentive to investment because of the gap between historical cost and replacement cost depreciation and because it probably adds to the uncertainty about the future course of business and profitability.

Possibly reflecting this fact, the market valuation of business assets today is low relative to their replacement cost. On balance, the 11.6 percent investment fraction may be regarded as possible, but it is certainly an optimistic assessment of future high-employment demand. Given the other sectoral projections, which are anchored to their actual 1977 surplus ratios, even this optimistic rate of business investment is sufficient to achieve high employment only with the federal high-employment deficit at 2.1 percent of GNP, or $42 billion in 1977 figures.

Achieving high employment by 1981 would allow time for some of the other sectoral projections to change. Column 8 differs from column 7 in projecting optimistic demands and sectoral surpluses. In particular: (1) investment demand is maintained at 11.6 percent; (2) the foreign surplus is reduced to 0.5 percent—a level that would be achieved by reducing the net export balance in the NIPA to zero; (3) state and local purchases are increased by enough to reduce the general funds surplus to zero; and (4) the historically low personal saving fraction that was projected in column 7 is maintained. In this case the high-employment economy is achieved with a balanced federal budget, which is calculated as the residual item in the column 8 sectoral projections.

The relevance of all this to the proposed tax cut is that the cut runs no realistic risk of being too large when viewed against the future requirements of fiscal policy. In Table 3 the high-employment budget was in surplus by 1981 with the tax cut. The analysis of Table 4 indicates that even with a balanced budget, unusually strong demand increases in other sectors would be required for high employment to be achieved. The Table 3 projections without the tax cut show a balanced budget at high employment by FY1979 and quickly growing surpluses thereafter. No prudent projection of demand in other sectors would make that a fiscal policy to be pursued at this time.

The Outlook for Inflation

The proposed tax cut makes good sense as fiscal policy when measured against goals for real GNP. Since the deep recession of 1974–1975, economic recovery has gradually reduced unemployment, and the outlook for further reductions is promising. But we are at least as far from eliminating inflation as we were in mid-1975. And neither the tax cut itself nor the economic outlook that goes with it offers any hope of slowing inflation in the near future. Expanding output and reducing unemployment have correctly been given top priority over this period, but there has been time to start dealing with inflation as well and, in particular, to start slowing inflation without compromising the goal of reducing unemployment.

Inflation is not being caused by excess demand, and the outlook is not for real gains so strong as to produce excess demand this year or next. The fiscal policy of which the tax cut is a part is not excessively expansionary. But economic policy is inadequate because it does not come to grips with the fact that today's chronic inflation is not rooted in the state of aggregate demand.

Tax cuts that are different from those being proposed but that provide an equivalent fiscal stimulus could have the double benefit of also helping to slow inflation. If employer payroll taxes were cut by $10 billion, business costs and prices would be reduced by 1 percent. A reduction of two percentage points in the employees' payroll tax would cost about $15 billion in revenue and might be offered in a bid to gain labor's cooperation in moderating wage increases. Tax reductions could be utilized as a bonus in a plan for rewarding moderation in wage and price increases, or in some other variant of a tax-based incomes policy.

Proposals such as these involve a loss of revenue and are thus relevant in any consideration of tax cuts. Because each of these proposals is flawed, each is easily dismissed, but an economic program without an effective plan for slowing inflation is more fatally flawed. The administration has announced a voluntary program for wage-price deceleration, but it would be highly optimistic to expect noticeable results from it. In this year's *Economic Report* the Council of Economic Advisers analyzes the problem of chronic inflation and outlines some ideas for trying to deal with it that promise to be effective. Until some such ideas become translated into policy proposals, the right grade in any evaluation of policy and the economic outlook must be "incomplete."

NOTES

[1] *The Budget of the United States Government, Fiscal Year 1979,* p. 41.

[2] For the late 1970s employment is considered to be "high" at a rate of 4.9 percent unemployment.

[3] Congressional Budget Office, *An Analysis of the President's Budgetary Proposals for Fiscal Year 1979, Staff Working Paper* (January 1, 1978).

[4] The swing would be a little less than the $18 billion deficit shown for FY1978 in line 3 because a small part of the tax cuts are included in the NIPA estimates for that year.

[5] *The Economic Report of the President* (January 1978), p. 87.

[6] Congressional Budget Office, *The Economic Outlook: A Report to the Senate and House Committees on the Budget,* Pt. II (February 1978), pp. 47–49.

[7] A current account "deficit," in conventional usage, contributes to a surplus in the foreign sector in the present accounting, which, in effect, takes the view of the foreigner; his purchases (our exports) add to total demand just as business investment or consumption spending does.

A Critique of Fiscal Policies Based on the Conventional Concept of Potential Output

William Fellner

Much of this paper will be concerned with the general macroeconomic concept underlying the 1979 budget. According to this concept, fiscal policy should be based on a specific way of estimating both the economy's output potential and the gap between its potential and its actual output. That gap should be eliminated even if speed limits need to be observed in achieving this result. According to the same concept, monetary policy should be required to promote such a course.

I believe that we shall be unable to straighten out our problems as long as we remain dedicated to this concept. On a macroeconomic level my main misgivings about the budget arise from my objections to this way of looking at the task of both fiscal and monetary policies, and a major purpose of this paper is to explain the reasons for my dissent as well as the bearing of this dissent on the 1979 budget.

The Concept of Potential Output

Despite some numerical differences, the macroeconomic concept underlying the 1979 budget represents the same general type of analysis as that presented in the 1977 Annual Report of the Ford administration's outgoing Council of Economic Advisers (CEA). The basic concept is also the same as that developed in the 1978 Annual Report of the new Carter CEA. This concept leads the expert to adopt a procedure—in my appraisal a misleading one—now widely used to compare the potential level of output toward which we should be moving with the actual output produced. The budget itself implies a somewhat more ambitious application of the procedure than does the analysis of the Carter CEA, which in turn presented a slightly more ambitious application than had the outgoing Ford CEA in January 1977.

Regardless of how ambitious the application, the basic procedure links three analytical steps, and I consider it essential to separate them. In one step an estimate is derived of the "normal" (long-run) growth rate in the neighborhood of which we are supposed to settle down after the cyclical recovery. A reasonable estimate of this growth rate is supposed to be about 3.5 percent annually. Such an estimate implies an increase in the labor force, a decline in the number of hours worked per week, and an increase in output per manhour. It is recognized by

---

The views in this paper are my own and do not necessarily reflect the views of the staff, advisory panels, officers or trustees of AEI.

policy advisers, present and past, as well as by the economics profession at large that such an estimate or guess may have to be adjusted as we go along, and with this qualification I too consider this a reasonable estimate. But the analytical step—and the operations leading to this estimate of a normal, post-recovery growth rate of about 3.5 percent—has practically no yield for the policy maker unless it is combined with two additional steps. One is required to estimate the *output base* from which the economy will tend to grow in the future at the estimated normal growth rate after completion of the cyclical recovery. Another is required to estimate the *speed* with which we should be moving toward that base.

In practice the question of the speed of movement toward the base for future normal growth is intimately connected with that of the height of the output base from which we are expected to move thereafter at, say, a 3.5 percent rate. This is because both the proposed speed of movement during the cyclical recovery and the post-recovery output base are likely to be closely connected with the size of the assumed present gap between the potential and the present actual output.

Once an expert has concluded that in 1978 we shall be, say, 4.5 percent below potential, he will be exceedingly likely to suggest a higher speed of cyclical recovery from 1978 to 1979 than if he had estimated the 1978 deficiency at, say, merely 1 percent. He is likely to propose a higher speed even though he will usually assume a later time of arrival at the potential level of output. In addition to recognizing this link between the proposed present speed and the size of the assumed gap, we need to recognize that in this framework a larger present gap usually implies a higher output base from which the economy will be growing at, say, about 3.5 percent after completion of the cyclical recovery. In this kind of framework a statement concerning the present gap implies a potential output expressed for each period by a point on a specified trend line that has been sloping upward for some time at a given yearly rate and that will continue to slope upward in the future. When actual output catches up with the reference trend line for potential output, the base for subsequent normal growth will be determined by the output indicated by that reference line for the time of catching up. A larger present gap usually results from the assumption of a steeper reference trend line in the now relevant range; and this implies that, at the time actual output catches up with potential, the output base for future normal growth will also be higher. To summarize, with a larger assumed present gap, the speed proposed for recovery will likely be greater, and usually the output base proposed for future normal growth will also be higher.

In view of the present expectations for the real GNP of 1978, the last Ford CEA's estimates of potential output would suggest that in 1978 we shall be about 4.3 percent below potential. In that CEA estimate the slope of the reference trend line determining the potential output was assumed to be 3.5 percent at present and in the coming years (0.1 percentage point lower than in the past fourteen years). The Carter CEA uses a slightly more ambitious version of the procedure, implying for the reference trend line at present and in the coming years a slope closer to 3.6 percent and suggesting a 1978 gap of about 4.5 percent. The budget documents do not specify the version of the procedure underlying the fiscal projections, but to make the projections internally consistent we need to interpret them as implying a version that is even more ambitious than that of the Carter CEA. On the assumption

12

that the reference trend line expressing the potential output has a 3.6 percent slope per year, the projected path of the actual output would catch up with the potential by late in 1981 (or perhaps very early in 1982), and at that time we should be expanding at a rate no higher than the normal growth rate. Yet the budget documents project for those years an actual growth rate that is very much higher than 3.6 percent: 5.0 percent for 1981 over 1980, 4.7 percent for 1982 over 1981, and 4.2 percent even for 1983 over 1982.

Although the budget projections are based on these assumptions, an attempt *has* been made to deemphasize the difference between the implications of the 1978 CEA projections and those in the budget documents. In its discussion accompanying the numerical budget projections, the administration recognizes the possible need to slow down to the long-run growth rate by late 1981 or early 1982. This is not consistent with the projections presented in the budget documents, but it would be approximately consistent with the view taken in the 1978 CEA report. Even this course raises the output base from which the economy would be growing in the future at its normal (long-run) rate, placing it slightly above the estimates made by the 1977 Ford CEA.

Despite these numerical differences, the various applications of the now conventional framework for determining the potential output have very much in common. The future normal growth rate is rather generally estimated to be in the neighborhood of 3.5 percent. Furthermore, in all these versions—including the 1977 estimates of the previous CEA—it is assumed that the reference trend line expressing the *potential* output has had just about this same slope for some time and that, aside from negligible differences, this slope will continue for some time to come. For a comparison of past years when, according to both the 1977 CEA and its successor, the actual output was close to the estimated potential—such as 1955, 1965, and 1973—the *actual* growth rate was, of course, about the same as the assumed potential growth rate, that is about 3.5 percent per year. Approximately this same rate has continued to be the growth rate of the *potential* output in these analyses, even though after 1973 the *actual* output had fallen significantly below this reference trend line. In other words, there has been no downward shift in the proper concept of the output base, from which the economy is to be interpreted as growing at the long-term growth rate after the cyclical recovery, despite the flare-up of inflation in the past decade and the adjustment process which this flare-up necessitated. Inflation and the subsequent readjustments have caused oscillations about the potential growth path but the experience of recent years is not supposed to have contradicted the assumption that the potential output path of the post-1973 period is a continuation of the earlier path of the potential. It is suggested that the procedure used also yields estimates of unemployment rates for the successive segments of the potential path of output, though not that the measured unemployment rates would have to remain constant along a given path.

Some of the details of this procedure could be adjusted in yet further versions of essentially the same analytical construct. But what could not be omitted from this general type of approach is the assumption that throughout the post-1973 adjustment period a monotonically rising potential output path is represented by a line that is the *continuation* of a monotonically upward sloping line originating in the pre-1973 era, even if the slope may occasionally change. Shifting the line down or up in view of the changing supply behavior of inputs does not fit into this framework.

Yet the post-1973 portion of that line is merely a figment of the imagination. Postulating that an allegedly well-defined pre-1973 line has continued through the post-1973 adjustment period and will continue into the future—and that this is the line with which we will have to catch up—is a misconception. The post-1973 portion of the line expressing the potential output gives the impression of being anchored in empirical research, but the truth of the matter is that it is anchored nowhere: it is floating in the air.

To be specific, the 1977 CEA analysis constructed the reference line in such a way that at the time of publication a measured unemployment rate of 4.9 percent and a measured capacity utilization rate of 85 percent corresponded to the potential. Some qualifying observations were added, and it was pointed out that according to some experts the unemployment rate corresponding to the potential could at that time have been slightly in excess of 5 percent rather than 4.9 percent. The 1978 CEA agrees with the 4.9 percent for 1977 but puts the measured unemployment corresponding to the potential output at 4.8 percent for the future period in which we are supposed to catch up with the potential. The budget documents project a potential output which implies an unemployment rate of 4.1 percent at the time of our catching up with the potential, but the subsequent discussion adds that 4.7 percent might prove the more realistic number. The 4.7 percent rate would correspond to a lower output base for future normal growth than would the 4.1 rate.

My misgivings relate not to this or that series of numbers but to the underlying concept which, I believe, might well prove to be our undoing unless it is abandoned in time. At present we know practically nothing about the measured unemployment rate along a future sustainable output path. Even if we do consider a future normal growth rate of roughly 3.5 percent to be a reasonable guess, we have no reason to couple this guess with an estimate of the measured unemployment rate that will prevail at the time when we need to slow down to this growth rate. Nor do we have reason to couple the 3.5 percent guess with an estimate of the output base from which we shall be growing at the future long-run rate. No package of such guesses or estimates is rooted in acceptable economic analysis; and some packages are all too likely to become points of departure for inflationary policy decisions that would prolong and sharpen our difficulties. The package of estimates I have surveyed, and particularly the projections underlying the budget message, are strongly suspect in this regard.

The Behavior of Price Levels

One of the essential things we do know about a sustainable output path is that from the value of the successive outputs along such a path it must be possible to recover the real supply prices of the inputs needed for producing the outputs. The real supply prices in question are those at which the inputs are voluntarily forthcoming. Further, we know that at any level of resource utilization the real supply prices of the inputs depend heavily on structural and institutional factors. Therefore the base from which we shall be able to grow at a long-run rate after the cyclical recovery also depends heavily on these factors and so does any reasonably defined potential output. These structural and institutional factors will determine the lowest sustainable level of measured unemployment, along with the highest sustainable output path.

To say that along the highest sustainable output path (with the lowest sustainable unemployment rate), the inputs must be forthcoming at their intended real supply prices implies that along a sustainable path market expectations concerning price-level behavior must be reasonably well geared to what the actual price-level behavior will be. If an output estimate does not recognize the need to gear price-level expectations to the price-level behavior that will in fact evolve, it may still prove to be a realistic output estimate for some specific year, but it is not an estimate of an output located along a sustainable path. Instead, such an estimate is a prediction of impending instability.

Decisive difficulties stand in the way of gearing market expectations to the kind of price-level behavior which develops when policy makers are trying to accommodate ("validate") the so-called basic rate of inflation that they believe they have detected in the data. One of the essential difficulties results from the complete lack of credibility of any suggestion that on the next occasion the same policy makers would abstain from accommodating a higher rate of inflation if they should happen to find a higher rate in the data and if an attempt to reduce that rate would be as inconvenient as would a policy that started moving gradually toward nonaccommodation right now. In such circumstances actual money-cost trends will steepen. They will come to reflect the expectation that the cost trends are autonomous, in the sense that policy makers will adjust the current-dollar effective demand to them rather than force an adjustment of the cost trends to the amount of current-dollar effective demand that is made available. Further, once the public has acquired enough experience with inflationary processes, money-cost trends are very likely to remind the public that accelerating inflation leads to recession, and in such an inflationary environment the recession may start at an earlier stage than would otherwise be the case.

This seems to be the main lesson to be derived from old and recent experience alike, but it is not the lesson which those responsible for the budget are trying to pass on to the public.

The Rate of Increase of Money GNP

From the macroeconomic point of view the main characteristic of the planned fiscal policy is that it proposes to utilize a large alleged gap between the potential and the present actual output. It is assumed that as a result of the large size of the gap the real GNP can continue to grow for many years at a highly supernormal, cyclical expansion rate. Despite the assumed large size of the gap, the rate of increase of the GNP deflator is assumed to creep upward in 1978 and then remain slightly higher in 1979 than it was in either 1976 or 1977; after that the inflation rate is expected to become gradually reduced, for reasons that are unexplained. The year-on-year rate of increase of the money GNP for 1978 over 1977 as well as for 1979 over 1978 is expected to be somewhat larger than it was in fact for 1977 over 1976. Even for 1980 over 1979 the rate of increase of money GNP is expected to be the same as it was for 1977 over 1976, though in the meantime we shall allegedly have had several years of real growth far in excess of the estimated long-run rate.

Past experience indicates a need for a continuous, gradual reduction of the rate of increase of the money GNP for two reasons: (1) establishing a sustainable path calls for a gradual reduction of the rate of increase of the real GNP toward the long-run rate; and (2) the same objective also calls for a gradual reduction of the inflation rate until practical stability of the price level is achieved (a condition exemplified by the behavior of prices from 1951 to 1965).

The objection that the policy of gradually but consistently reducing the rate of increase of money GNP would have to cause a recession is unconvincing. A firm and credible policy line of this kind would significantly influence price expectations and thereby influence money-cost trends at all levels of activity, not merely at recession levels. No one could, of course, guarantee a "recessionproof" economy on the way toward price stability, but any recession encountered on the way would at least clear the ground for subsequent healthy growth. In contrast, a road marked by successive flare-ups of inflation is certain to bring increasingly severe recessions which do not clear the ground for desirable trends. A policy of continued accommodation of already observed inflationary tendencies would predictably put us on that road.

So much for the general economic projections into which the budgetary plans are made to fit. As for the budget figures proper, their inflationary character is seen, for example, in the fact that for the time being the deficit is not expected to decline in a period of pronounced cyclical recovery. There do exist constructive tax-reduction packages that would have been compatible with a consistent move toward budgetary balance as the cyclical expansion progresses. For instance, prompt indexation of the individual income tax along with a gradual phasing in of two investment-promoting measures—the exemption of inflationary revaluations from corporate taxation and the abolition of the double taxation of dividends—could have been made consistent with moving toward budgetary balance during the expansion. This is true all the more because fiscal savings could be achieved in the many cases in which government programs do not serve their avowed purpose effectively. As an illustration, it seems very likely that less expensive and much better focused on-the-job training programs would serve the objective of a reasonable manpower policy better than the exceedingly costly job programs which have emerged.

In general, it is difficult to avoid the impression that our policy makers have not shelved the hypothesis of the Phillips trade-off and that even more than the experience of the past years will be needed to achieve that result. Yet it is getting late.

16

Summary of Discussion

Although there were many areas of agreement between Fellner and Perry, there was clear disagreement over the probable effectiveness of different policy options for reducing the rate of inflation. While Perry agreed that Fellner's proposal for gradually reducing the rate of growth of money GNP might have some beneficial impact on inflation rates, he did not believe that this could be accomplished without doing great harm to the rate of growth of real GNP. Fellner replied that if it were clear to investors and consumers that fiscal and monetary policy would take a sufficiently hard-boiled approach to inflation, there would be a reduction in inflationary expectations that would greatly limit the temporary slowing of real economic activity. However, Fellner added, no one could guarantee that the economy would be recessionproof on the way to price stability. The difference is that any recession encountered on the way to a stable price level would provide a foundation for "subsequent, healthy, normal growth," while a policy of accommodating again and again the so-called underlying inflation rates of successive periods leads inevitably to recessions of increasing severity which do not even clear the ground for healthy growth.

Just as Perry doubted that Fellner's proposed reduction in the growth of money GNP could be effective without imposing great costs, Fellner questioned Perry's favorable comments on plans such as that proposed by Arthur Okun which would provide tax benefits as a reward for price and wage constraint. Perry's paper admitted that such plans were flawed but implied that the administration's macro policy was also flawed because it contained no plan to curb inflation other than the deceleration policy which is unlikely to be effective.

Much of the remaining discussion focused on the concept of potential GNP, which Fellner had criticized in detail. Michael Boskin and Norman Ture argued strongly that estimates of potential GNP had to take account of the supply responses of different factors of production to tax and other policy variables. Perry accepted the theoretical merits of this argument but suggested that, as a practical matter, such responses were likely to be very small and that great harm was not done if they were ignored.

James Buchanan argued that Fellner, Boskin, and Ture missed an important point in criticizing the estimates and forecasts of institutions such as the Council of Economic Advisers and the Congressional Budget Office. He suggested that the technicians making such estimates operated within severe political constraints which forced them to provide a rationale for whatever fiscal policy happened to be politically popular.

Martin Bailey noted the importance of Fellner's point that the administration's estimate of potential GNP was based on an assumed unemployment rate of 4.9 percent in 1977 whereas the administration's budget projections assumed that a 4.1

percent unemployment rate could be attained in 1983. Bailey asked Perry whether he thought 4.1 was attainable. Perry replied that he did not think it to be a realistic benchmark. Darwin Johnson of the Office of Management and Budget said that it was necessary to differentiate between the unemployment rate assumed for the statistical purposes of estimating high-employment GNP and the administration's eventual target of 4.0 percent unemployment by the end of 1983 which is consistent with the goal of the Humphrey-Hawkins bill.

Van Ooms asked Fellner if he shared Perry's view that the substitution of payroll tax cuts for income tax cuts would have a beneficial impact on inflation. Fellner agreed that the payroll tax on employers was probably shifted forward in the form of price increases. Richard Musgrave supported this view, but it was questioned by Attiat Ott and Jude Wanniski who doubted that there was a difference between the shifting of payroll taxes and of income taxes on wages. Perry emphasized that he was considering the short-run incidence of the payroll tax as it affected prices and not incidence in the long run as it affected relative shares. He suggested that short-run incidence was important because any short-run increase in prices was likely to be built into the long-run inflation rate.

James Wetzler asked why neither Fellner nor Perry emphasized the potential role of monetary policy. He suggested that we could move toward a balanced budget in the long run while relying on the monetary authorities to provide the stimulus necessary for maintaining the recovery. Fellner agreed that monetary policy was vital to the long-run economic outlook while fiscal policy has its main impact in the short run. He worried that the administration was relying on a monetary policy that would accommodate fiscal policy in the short run and suggested that we would be better off with a stable long-run monetary strategy that was not destabilized by fiscal policy considerations.

Musgrave expressed strong support for Fellner's desire to index the tax system for inflation. He argued that indexation would eliminate the "free ride" which allows the government to raise the ratio of spending to GNP without explicitly raising tax rates. As a result of indexation, he suggested that in public discussion debate regarding the appropriate size of the government sector would be more clearly differentiated from debate regarding the relation between spending and tax levels necessary for an appropriate stabilization policy.

PART TWO

THE PERSONAL INCOME TAX

The 1978 Personal Income Tax Program

Emil M. Sunley

The President's tax program recommends a gross tax reduction for individuals of $23.5 billion. Offset against this is $6.8 billion in long-needed structural reforms. The net reduction for individuals is $16.8 billion for calendar year 1979. The reductions in tax will begin to be reflected in take-home pay beginning in October 1978.

Distribution of Individual Tax Cuts

In proposing this substantial income tax relief, the administration recommends a more equitable allocation of the tax burden. The President is committed to the principle that the net tax reductions should be focused on those who need tax relief the most—low- and middle-income Americans—and a combination of tax cuts and reforms provides sizable reductions for these taxpayers. (See Tables 1 and 2.)

TABLE 1

EXPANDED INCOME AND TAX LIABILITY UNDER PRESENT LAW AND PROPOSALS
FOR RATE REDUCTION AND THE REFORM OF PERSONAL INCOME TAX
(money amounts in millions of dollars)

Expanded Income Class[a]	Number of Returns (thousands)	Expanded Income	Present Law		Administration Proposal	
			Tax liability	Effective tax rate (percent)	Tax liability	Effective tax rate (percent)
Less than $5,000	25,474	57,557	141	0.2	−251	−0.4
$5–10,000	20,109	149,590	8,227	5.5	6,368	4.3
$10–15,000	16,106	201,036	18,071	9.0	15,361	7.6
$15–20,000	11,824	205,086	23,009	11.2	20,148	9.8
$20–30,000	9,907	237,041	32,778	13.8	29,593	12.5
$30–50,000	3,347	124,836	22,017	17.6	20,971	16.8
$50–100,000	985	67,484	16,492	24.4	16,344	24.2
$100–200,000	198	27,371	8,084	29.5	8,261	30.2
More than $200,000	49	21,573	6,476	30.0	6,838	31.7
Total (average rates)	87,998	1,091,573	135,293	(12.4)	123,633	(11.3)

a 1976 levels of income.

NOTE: Columns may not add up to totals because of rounding.

SOURCE: Office of the Secretary of the Treasury, Office of Tax Analysis.

TABLE 2

Personal Income Tax Liabilities: Present Law and Administration Proposal

	Present Law		Administration Proposal		Tax Change	
Expanded Income Class[a]	Tax liability (millions of dollars)	Percentage distribution (percent)	Tax liability (millions of dollars)	Percentage distribution (percent)	Tax liability (millions of dollars)	Change as percent of present law tax (percent)
Less than $5,000	141	0.1	−251	−0.2	−392	278.0
$5–10,000	8,227	6.1	6,368	5.2	−1,859	−22.6
$10–15,000	18,071	13.4	15,361	12.4	−2,710	−15.0
$15–20,000	23,009	17.0	20,148	16.3	−2,861	−12.4
$20–30,000	32,778	24.2	29,593	23.9	−3,185	−9.7
$30–50,000	22,017	16.3	20,971	17.0	−1,046	−4.8
$50–100,000	16,492	12.2	16,344	13.2	−148	−0.9
$100–200,000	8,084	6.0	8,261	6.7	177	2.2
More than $200,000	6,476	4.8	6,838	5.5	362	5.6
Total	135,293	100.0	123,633	100.0	−11,660	−8.6

[a] 1976 levels of income.

Note: Columns may not add up to totals because of rounding.

Source: Office of the Secretary of the Treasury, Office of Tax Analysis.

The administration's program reduces taxes for most high-income taxpayers as well, but it increases liabilities for some persons who now use unjustified tax preferences to escape paying their fair share of taxes.

Over 94 percent of the income tax relief is provided to families making less than $30,000, but families in every income class through $100,000 will enjoy a tax cut. The net tax reductions are proportionately largest at the low end of the income scale. For example, families earning between $5,000 and $10,000 will have their taxes reduced by 22.6 percent; those earning $20,000 to $30,000 will have a 9.7 percent reduction; and for those earning more than $100,000, tax liabilities will be raised by a modest 3.7 percent. In dollar terms, the typical family earning $20,000 a year will save $270 in taxes; an average family with $100,000 of income will pay $590 more. The share of the total income tax burden borne by taxpayers with incomes under $30,000 falls from 60.8 to 57.6 percent.

The carefully designed net tax reduction of $25 billion for businesses and individuals is the centerpiece of the administration's economic program. These tax reductions will sustain the current economic recovery. The individual tax cuts of $16.8 billion will maintain consumer purchasing power by offsetting both the scheduled increase in the social security tax and the impact of inflation on effective tax rates. The ratio of personal taxes and employee social security taxes to personal income in 1979 will be brought down to 14.1 percent, which is below the 1977 level of 14.3 percent. Without the proposed tax cut, the ratio would rise at least one full percentage point.

$240 per Capita Credit and Rate Cuts

As shown in Table 3, the major elements in the tax programs are a reduction in tax rates and the substitution of a $240 personal credit for personal exemptions under present law. For joint returns the new rates will range from 12 percent for the first $1,000 of taxable income to 68 percent on taxable income in excess of $200,000. The new schedule of rates takes two percentage points off present rates at both the bottom and the top of the income scale. In the lower middle of the joint return schedule, $12,000 to $24,000 of taxable income, the rates are cut up to five percentage points.

The proposed $240 credit will replace the current $750 exemption for each family member and the general tax credit, which is now equal to the greater of $35 per taxpayer and dependent or 2 percent at the first $9,000 of taxable income. The existing tax benefits for family members vary directly in proportion to income level. A family of four in the 50 percent tax bracket ($46,000 of taxable income) now enjoys a tax saving of $1,680 from exemptions and the general credit while a family in the 22 percent bracket ($10,000) saves slightly more than a third of that. By contrast, the $240 credit will provide a tax saving of $960 to a four-member family regardless of the income level. In large part because of this new credit, the tax-free level of income for a family of four will rise to $9,256 under the tax program from $7,200 under current law.

The per capita credit is being proposed in combination with a restructuring of tax rates. For a four-person family with less than $20,000 of income, the $240 credit will provide greater tax savings than would the existing personal exemption and general tax credit, even if no changes were made in the tax rate schedule. Families with more than $20,000 of income, however, are not going to be worse off under the administration's proposal. The proposed rate schedules have been designed to offset the tax increases that would occur at high-income levels if a $240 credit simply replaced the existing personal exemption and general tax credit. For most taxpayers the rate cuts also offset the effects on tax liabilities of the administration's reforms. These reforms have two objectives: simplification and equity.

Simplification

Simplification is the primary objective of the repeal of the deductibility of state and local gasoline taxes, sales taxes, and miscellaneous taxes; the repeal of the deduction for political contributions, and the revision of the deductibility of medical and casualty expenses. These proposals continue the simplification efforts of last year's Tax Reduction and Simplification Act. The percentage of taxpayers who take the flat standard deduction will be increased from 76 to 84 percent.

The benefit of deducting gasoline and sales taxes is slight for even the 23 percent of the taxpayers who itemize. Most taxpayers determine the amount to be deducted from tables accompanying the tax forms, and the effect on tax liabilities is sufficiently uniform that deductibility is equivalent to an adjustment in tax rates. The administration is proposing just such an adjustment.

Repeal of the deduction for political contributions is proposed because the credit in present law makes the deduction redundant. In a society which honors the principle of one man, one vote, there is less justification for this deduction than for the credit.

TABLE 3

Estimated Tax Changes Resulting from Proposed Rate Reduction and Reform of Personal Income Tax, by Expanded Income Classes
(millions of dollars)

Tax Change	Less than $5,000	$5–10,000
$240 personal credit and reduced tax rates	−423	−2,008
Repeal alternative tax on capital gains	—	—
Change in minimum tax	—	—
Repeal gasoline tax deduction	—	15
Repeal sales tax deduction	1	26
Repeal miscellaneous taxes and political contribution deduction	—	6
Change in medical and casualty deduction	1	41
Tax interest element of annuity contracts	5	—
Individual real estate shelters	3	4
Taxable municipal bonds	3	30
Taxation of unemployment compensation payments	—	—
Nondiscrimination rule for health and group term life plans	2	2
Limit tax credits to 90 percent of tax liability	—	2
Taxation of qualified retirement plans	—	—
Total	−392	−1,859

— Less than $500,000.

a Expanded income consists of adjusted gross income plus individual tax preferences subject to present law minimum tax less interest expense (other than home mortgage interest) to the extent of investment income.

Note: Columns may not add to totals because of rounding.

Source: Office of the Secretary of the Treasury, Office of Tax Analysis.

On Form 1040 Schedule A there are now twelve lines for deducting medical expenses and six for deducting casualty losses. It is proposed that deductions for uninsured medical expenses and casualty losses (in excess of $100) be combined in a new "hardship expense" deduction. Only hardship expenses in excess of 10 percent of adjusted gross income would be deductible. Medical insurance premiums and medicines will be treated the same as other medical expenses. In this manner, preparation of tax returns will be simplified greatly, and the deduction will be available only to taxpayers whose ability to pay has been affected significantly by medical and casualty costs.

As Table 3 indicates, these changes will bring in $4 billion. The proposed rate schedules, as I indicated earlier, are designed to offset the tax increases from pruning itemized deductions. The deeper rate cuts in the middle-income range ensure that few itemizers will have a tax increase.

Equity

The primary equity reforms add $2.8 billion to personal tax liabilities. Some of the proposals, however, are of greater consequence than the changes in liabilities would

	Expanded Income Class[a]							
$10–15,000	$15–20,000	$20–30,000	$30–50,000	$50–100,000	$100–200,000	More than $200,000	Total
−3,149	−3,587	−4,687	−2,215	−879	−216	−143	−17,305
—	—	—	—	13	46	52	113
—	—	—	—	4	47	177	229
63	113	210	124	45	10	3	582
116	236	516	417	248	79	32	1,672
29	50	94	81	58	33	35	386
143	237	401	308	173	53	39	1,396
10	15	55	64	64	49	58	320
4	7	12	48	73	68	100	320
45	38	74	52	6	2	5	255
2	11	95	101	55	11	—	275
2	2	4	5	5	4	4	29
7	6	10	6	3	2	1	38
—	—	—	8	9	4	9	30
−2,710	−2,861	−3,185	−1,046	−148	177	362	−11,660

suggest. Also at stake in these reforms is the efficiency with which economic activity is conducted.

Advancing beyond the closing of tax shelters in the Tax Reform Act of 1976, the administration recommends that accelerated depreciation of structures other than low-income housing be phased out. Generally, the proposal would require taxpayers to depreciate buildings for tax purposes in equal annual charges over average tax lives now used for the various classes of structures. The tax program also extends the "at risk" rule, restricts the use of limited partnerships, implements auditing of partnerships, taxes annuity interest in the year it is earned, and eliminates the possibility of offsetting half of regular tax liability in the computation of minimum tax.

The administration is proposing to terminate the alternative tax on capital gains. The effect of the current provision is to grant taxpayers in the highest income bracket an additional tax preference over and above the regular exclusion of one-half of capital gains. Through the alternative tax, individuals above the 50 percent bracket can take advantage of a 25 percent ceiling on the first $50,000 of capital gains. Taxpayers with incomes over $200,000 can use the alternative tax to exclude in effect nearly 65 percent of $50,000 of capital gains each year. A family with $50,000 of income can exclude only half of capital gains.

Two of the reforms proposed will reduce the opportunities for employers to discriminate among employees in distributing fringe benefits. The first would extend to employer medical, disability, and group life insurance plans the anti-discrimination rules that now apply to company retirement and legal plans. The second would change the rules under which qualified retirement plans may integrate with social security. The proposed rules would assure that, if a company provides a pension for any employee, it must make substantial provision for every employee not represented by a collective bargaining unit.

The administration proposes taxation of unemployment compensation received by taxpayers with adjusted gross income plus unemployment compensation above $20,000 for single and $25,000 for married taxpayers. The inclusion would be phased in at fifty cents on the dollar. Thus, a single taxpayer with $19,000 of adjusted gross income under present law and $2,000 of unemployment compensation would be taxed on $500 (half of $1,000) of his unemployment compensation. The proposal will mainly affect unemployment recipients with substantial income from investments or married to a spouse with earned income.

The administration also proposes to revise the tax treatment of interest on state and local government debt. Repeal of tax exemption is proposed only for pollution control bonds and bonds for the development of industrial parks and unneeded private hospitals. The main element in the proposal is to offer state and local government borrowers the option of a subsidy on taxable bonds issued; they may continue to issue tax-exempt bonds. The proposal actually will make it possible for state and local governments to borrow at lower net interest costs than tax exemption alone would permit. On reasonable assumptions, state and local borrowing costs will be reduced about 15 percent whether financing is through taxable or tax-exempt bonds. And the equity of the personal income tax will be improved since the implicit tax paid by holders of tax-exempt bonds will be increased.

Social Security Taxes and Inflation

For most taxpayers, there will be a net reduction in combined income and payroll tax liability through 1979 even after the scheduled social security tax increases. Tables 4 and 5 compare the combined income and social security taxes under 1977 law with the proposed law for 1978 and 1979. Included in the calculations are the social security tax increases resulting from legislation enacted prior to 1977 as well as the increases contained in the Social Security Amendments of 1977. The tables assume a four-person, one-earner family with wage income at various levels. The recommended income tax cuts will completely offset the increase in social security taxes for families with wage income up to $25,000 in 1978 and $20,000 in 1979. A substantial offset will result even above those levels. Tables 6 and 7 present similar information for a four-person, two-earner family in which it is assumed that each spouse earns half the total family income.

Table 8 exhibits for 1977 and 1979 the combined effects at various income levels of social security taxes, inflation, and the proposed tax cuts of the President.

26

TABLE 4

COMBINED INCOME TAX AND SOCIAL SECURITY TAX BURDENS
FOR FOUR-PERSON, ONE-EARNER FAMILIES, 1978
(dollars)

	Present Law Tax			1978 Proposed Tax			Change in Tax		
Wage Income	Income tax[a]	Social security tax[b]	Total tax	Income tax[a]	Social security tax[c]	Total tax	Income tax	Social security tax	Total tax
5,000	− 300	292	− 8	− 300	303	3	0	11	11
10,000	446	585	1,031	192	605	797	− 254	20	− 234
15,000	1,330	877	2,207	1,166	908	2,074	− 164	31	− 133
20,000	2,180	965	3,145	2,042	1,071	3,113	− 138	106	− 32
25,000	3,150	965	4,115	3,025	1,071	4,096	− 125	106	− 19
30,000	4,232	965	5,197	4,150	1,071	5,221	− 82	106	24
40,000	6,848	965	7,813	6,748	1,071	7,819	− 100	106	6
50,000	9,950	965	10,915	9,855	1,071	10,926	− 95	106	11
100,000	28,880	965	29,845	28,640	1,071	29,711	− 240	106	− 134

[a] Assumes deductible expenses equal to 23 percent of income.

[b] Calculated under prior law rate and base for 1977 (5.85 percent and $16,500), employees' share only.

[c] Calculated under present law rate and base for 1978 (6.05 percent and $17,700), employees' share only.

SOURCE: Office of the Secretary of the Treasury, Office of Tax Analysis.

Taxes in 1977 reflect social security and income tax liabilities calculated under the tax law then in effect for income levels which are equivalent in real terms to somewhat higher income levels in 1979. Taxes in 1979 for these higher income levels are based on the social security taxes that would then apply and the administration's proposed income tax reductions.

The effective tax rate—that is, the combined income and social security taxes as a percentage of the appropriate income level—is calculated for each year. If the combined effective tax rate remains constant, the real tax burden of taxpayers does not change. For example, if nominal income rises by, say, 6 percent, taxes will also rise by 6 percent, and the *after-tax* income of the taxpayer will increase by 6 percent as well, leaving him exactly as well off in real terms (that is, adjusted for the price increase). Similarly, an increase in the combined effective tax rate means that the taxpayer is worse off in real terms because his tax has increased by a greater percentage than has his income. With a decrease in the effective tax rate, the taxpayer is of course better off in real terms.

The President's tax proposals are designed to provide sufficient stimulus to maintain the current economic recovery while at the same time keeping the size of the deficit manageable. In achieving these objectives, the tax program illustrated in Table 8 has also lowered the real tax burden of four-person families with less than $17,000 of income. Even at $30,000 of income, the increase in the effective tax rate is less than one percentage point, and this is due to the increases in social security enacted by Congress last year.

This trade-off of income tax reductions for social security tax increases should not be viewed as essentially a tax equity issue. The social security tax is more nearly a benefit tax than is the federal personal income tax. Each person in paying his social security tax buys on the terms currently being offered a benefit for himself and his family. The increase in social security taxes enacted last year was intended explicitly to preserve the real value of benefits promised for future payment. Unless and until the basic rationale of social security is changed, each taxpayer has a personal stake in the financing of the system.

The basic consideration in the design of the federal personal income tax is a fair allocation of the burdens of financing the provision of public goods. Thus, the major policy issue is the distribution of the tax burden. Reducing personal income taxes to compensate families for inflation is primarily a device to promote economic stabilization. The choice is between automatic tax cuts or periodic ones. Periodic or discretionary tax cuts may have an advantage since an unindexed personal income tax builds into the federal fiscal system an anti-inflationary bias that would otherwise be lacking.

TABLE 5

COMBINED INCOME TAX AND SOCIAL SECURITY TAX BURDENS
FOR FOUR-PERSON, ONE-EARNER FAMILIES, 1979

(dollars)

	Present Law Tax			1979 Proposed Tax			Change in Tax		
Wage Income	Income tax[a]	Social security tax[b]	Total tax	Income tax[c]	Social security tax[d]	Total tax	Income tax	Social security tax	Total tax
5,000	−300	292	−8	−300	306	6	0	14	14
10,000	446	585	1,031	134	613	747	−312	28	−284
15,000	1,330	877	2,207	1,072	919	1,991	−258	42	−216
20,000	2,180	965	3,145	1,910	1,226	3,136	−270	261	−9
25,000	3,150	965	4,115	2,830	1,404	4,234	−320	439	119
30,000	4,232	965	5,197	3,910	1,404	5,314	−322	439	117
40,000	6,848	965	7,813	6,630	1,404	8,034	−218	439	221
50,000	9,950	965	10,915	9,870	1,404	11,274	−80	439	359
100,000	28,880	965	29,845	29,470	1,404	30,874	590	439	1,029

[a] Assumes deductible expenses equal to 23 percent of income under present law.

[b] Calculated under prior law rate and base for 1977 (5.85 percent and $16,500), employees' share only.

[c] Assumes deductible expenses equal to 20 percent of income under proposal.

[d] Calculated under present law rate and base for 1979 (6.13 percent and $22,900), employees' share only.

SOURCE: Office of the Secretary of the Treasury, Office of Tax Analysis.

28

TABLE 6

Combined Income Tax and Social Security Tax Burdens for Four-Person, Two-Earner Families, 1978

(dollars)

Wage Income	Present Law Tax			1978 Proposed Tax			Change in Tax		
	Income tax[a]	Social security tax[b]	Total tax	Income tax[a]	Social security tax[c]	Total tax	Income tax	Social security tax	Total tax
5,000	−300	292	−8	−300	303	3	0	11	11
10,000	446	585	1,031	192	605	797	−254	20	−234
15,000	1,330	877	2,207	1,166	908	2,074	−164	31	−133
20,000	2,180	1,170	3,350	2,042	1,210	3,252	−138	40	−98
25,000	3,150	1,463	4,613	3,025	1,513	4,538	−125	50	−75
30,000	4,232	1,755	5,987	4,150	1,815	5,965	−82	60	−22
40,000	6,848	1,931	8,779	6,748	2,142	8,890	−100	211	111
50,000	9,950	1,931	11,881	9,855	2,142	11,997	−95	211	116
100,000	28,880	1,931	30,811	28,640	2,142	30,782	−240	211	−29

[a] Assumes deductible expenses equal to 23 percent of income.

[b] Calculated under prior law rate and base for 1977 (5.85 percent and $16,500), employees' share only.

[c] Calculated under present law rate and base for 1978 (6.05 percent and $17,700), employees' share only.

NOTE: It is assumed that each spouse earns 50 percent of total family income.

SOURCE: Office of the Secretary of the Treasury, Office of Tax Analysis.

TABLE 7

Combined Income Tax and Social Security Tax Burdens for Four-Person, Two-Earner Families, 1979

(dollars)

Income Wage	Present Law Tax			1979 Proposed Tax			Change in Tax		
	Income tax[a]	Social security tax[b]	Total tax	Income tax[c]	Social security tax[d]	Total tax	Income tax	Social security tax	Total tax
5,000	−300	292	−8	−300	306	6	0	14	14
10,000	446	585	1,031	134	613	747	−312	28	−284
15,000	1,330	877	2,207	1,072	919	1,991	−258	42	−216
20,000	2,180	1,170	3,350	1,910	1,226	3,136	−270	56	−214
25,000	3,150	1,463	4,613	2,830	1,533	4,363	−320	70	−250
30,000	4,232	1,755	5,987	3,910	1,839	5,749	−322	84	−238
40,000	6,848	1,931	8,779	6,630	2,452	9,082	−218	521	303
50,000	9,950	1,931	11,881	9,870	2,808	12,678	−80	877	797
100,000	28,880	1,931	30,811	29,470	2,808	32,278	590	877	1,467

[a] Assumes deductible expenses equal to 23 percent of income under present law.

[b] Calculated under prior law rate and base for 1977 (5.85 percent and $16,500), employees' share only.

[c] Assumes deductible expenses equal to 20 percent of income under proposal.

[d] Calculated under present law rate and base for 1979 (6.13 percent and $22,900), employees' share only.

NOTE: It is assumed that each spouse earns 50 percent of total family income.

SOURCE: Office of the Secretary of the Treasury, Office of Tax Analysis.

TABLE 8

INCOME AND SOCIAL SECURITY TAXES IN 1977 LAW AND PROPOSED 1979 LAW:
THE EFFECT OF CHANGES ON EFFECTIVE TAX RATES FOR FOUR-PERSON,
ONE-EARNER FAMILIES
(money amounts in dollars)

| 1979 Income Level | 1977 Taxes[a] | | | | | 1979 Taxes | | | | Change in Tax | | |
	Equivalent 1977 income[b]	Income tax[c]	Social security tax[d]	Total tax	Combined effective tax rate (percent)	Income tax[c]	Social security tax[e]	Total tax	Combined effective tax rate (percent)	Combined Tax Liability with 1977 Effective Tax Rate	Amount	Effective tax rate (percent)
5,000	4,440	−356	260	−96	−2.16	−300	306	6	0.12	−108	114[f]	2.28
10,000	8,880	259	519	778	8.76	134	613	747	7.47	876	−129	−1.29
12,000	10,656	567	623	1,190	11.17	502	736	1,238	10.31	1,340	−102	−0.85
15,000	13,320	1,070	779	1,849	13.88	1,072	920	1,992	13.28	2,082	−90	−0.60
17,000	15,096	1,345	883	2,228	14.75	1,430	1,042	2,472	14.34	2,509	−37	−0.20
20,000	17,759	1,788	965	2,753	15.50	1,910	1,226	3,136	15.68	3,100	36	0.18
25,000	22,199	2,603	965	3,568	16.07	2,830	1,404	4,234	16.94	4,018	216	0.86
30,000	26,639	3,503	965	4,468	16.77	3,910	1,404	5,314	17.71	5,032	282	0.94
40,000	35,519	5,606	965	6,571	18.50	6,630	1,404	8,034	20.08	7,400	634	1.59

[a] Tax law in effect December 31, 1977.

[b] Assumes a 12.6 percent increase from 1977 to 1979.

[c] Assumes itemized deductions equal to 23 percent of gross income in 1977 and 20 percent of gross income under the proposed 1979 law.

[d] Calculated under 1977 wage base ($16,500) and tax rate (5.85 percent), employees' share only.

[e] Calculated under 1979 wage base ($22,900) and tax rate (6.13 percent), employees' share only.

[f] Under the administration's welfare proposal, taxpayers in this income class will have a net tax reduction from the liberalized earned income credit.

SOURCE: Office of the Secretary of the Treasury, Office of Tax Analysis.

Cutting and
Reforming the Personal Income Tax

David F. Bradford

Although we have learned a lot and are getting better at thinking through the economics of tax policy issues, there remain great gaps in our understanding of the effect of taxes and limitations in our ability to structure the debate on tax policy issues. As an illustration, my task and preparation would have been different if the topic had been "Cutting and Reforming the Taxation of Persons" instead of "Cutting and Reforming the Personal Income Tax." Better, I think, would have been something like "Cutting and Reforming the Burden of Federal Expenditures on Persons." Let me begin by setting the subject of tax cuts in this, its proper context.

If the usual budget totals are accepted as a convenient measure of the extent of government expenditure, and if the ratio of these to total output in the economy is regarded as a way of normalizing for income, population, and price changes, there does appear to be some cutting of the burden of federal expenditures in the budget, but the amount is small. For example, according to the budget document, the ratio of total budget outlays to GNP will have gone from 21.9 percent in FY1977 to 22.6 percent in 1978 and will go back down to 22.0 percent in 1979—though all these figures are a notch higher than the level of 19.8 percent in 1974. If instead purchases of goods and services by the federal government are taken as a measure of expenditure (using projections made on the basis of national income accounts given in the *Economic Report of the President, 1978*), and if share of GNP is again used as an index of size of the "burden," the corresponding percentages are much smaller but they move in a similar way—7.7 percent in FY1977 and 1978; 7.6 percent expected for FY1979—and they are about the same as the 7.7 percent in FY1974.

Presumably indicators such as these should be examined in analyzing "cuts" in burdens, and not the announced $18.3 billion reduction, almost 9 percent, in individual income tax receipts budgeted for FY1979 nor even the $24.3 billion (5.2 percent) reduction in tax receipts from all the proposed tax changes embodied in the Carter budget. As long as the expenditure totals are held constant, the total tax change merely affects the residual which is to be financed by the issue of debt. (I am completely neglecting here the problem of organizing these financing arrangements to achieve objectives of macroeconomic stabilization.)

These tax data and the corresponding national debt data, together with information about the transfer programs of the federal government, might be expected to form a starting point for an analysis of the differences in the distribution of burdens among alternative financing programs. Naturally our interest is in the comparison of the President's tax program with current policy. If the expenditure side is held fixed, these alternatives might be described in aggregate terms by Table 1.

These summary statistics indicate clearly how important it is to look beyond the details of the proposed changes in individual income tax rules to get an idea of what the overall program of financing decisions will do to the distribution of the burden of government expenditures. For example, the difference in deficit between $36.2 billion in current policy figures and $60.6 billion in the Carter budget roughly equals the difference between $214.0 billion and $190.1 billion in individual income taxes. Some persons must bear the burden of this debt difference. In other words, a new, largely unknown burden is imposed by the increasing debt just as the individual income tax burden is being reduced by a comparable magnitude. Yet it is the income tax changes that receive all the attention. A second example is the corporation income tax cut of $6.4 billion from $68.9 billion to $62.5 billion in the Carter budget. Again, this significant change has implications for who will bear the burden of government expenditure, and these effects ought to be built into our thinking about tax policy.

The rub, of course, is that we have only a very imperfect understanding of how changes in these elements of the financing structure affect the distribution of burden. Anyone who has looked into the literature knows about the controversies surrounding the incidence of both the corporation income tax and the government debt issue. I am not going to offer any new insights into those questions, but I do think it important to acknowledge the tremendous quantitative significance of the parts of the financing picture about which we are ignorant. Looking at tables of changes in the individual income tax burden as a way of understanding distributional effects is a little bit like examining only the wind damage figures in the aftermath of a combination hurricane and flood.

A step that would assist rational discussion of these issues would be to adopt some terms other than "personal" and "business" to categorize tax components, as

TABLE 1
FY1979 FINANCING BY SOURCE
(billions of dollars)

Source	Current Policy	Carter Budget
Individual income tax	214.0	190.1
Corporation income tax	68.9	62.5
Social insurance taxes and contributions	141.9	141.9
Excise taxes	18.7	25.5
Other taxes, duties and miscellaneous receipts	20.5	19.7
Deficit	36.2	60.6
Outlays	500.2	500.2

SOURCE: Figures are derived from Congressional Budget Office, *An Analysis of the President's Budgetary Proposals for Fiscal Year 1979*; Carter budget totals include effects of energy taxes and rebates.

though business taxes were not also borne by persons. (It would also be desirable to resist the tendency to equate "business" with "corporate." The sum of "proprietors' income" and "rental income of persons" in the national income accounts is estimated at $123.2 billion for 1977, almost as large as the $140.3 billion of corporate profits.)

A final note in this extended prologue: We should recognize that there is even room for debate about who bears income taxes. One reason, for example, that we are not sure how the corporation income tax affects the distribution of burdens is that we are not sure how it affects the levels of wages and interest. The same problem arises with respect to the taxation of returns to saving at the individual level, and the same sort of observation applies with respect to the effect of individual taxes on the decision of different household members to enter the labor market and the amount and quality of the services they offer there.

This said, let us proceed to examine the proposed changes in the individual income tax by looking first at changes in the way families are to be treated and at the overall progressivity of the proposals and then at some of the specific issues of income definition and tax expenditure. At the end of the paper I shall return to some general comments about the missing items in the debate.

Structure and Progressivity

Much is made in the administration materials of the change sought to use a tax credit instead of an exemption to make the basic adjustment for family size. The Council of Economic Advisers recently asserted: "The *most fundamental change* proposed in the Individual Income Tax is the replacement of the $750 personal exemption and the general tax credit with a single per capita tax of $240." [1] Since I do not have a strong intuition about the right way to tax families, I am rather surprised at the emphasis on this change in the administration's proposals.

There appears to be considerable confusion about the connection between the shift to a credit and the progressivity of the tax change. As will be clear to a careful reader of the Treasury materials or the Council's report, the choice between a credit and an exemption is *not* one between a more or less progressive tax system—especially since changes are being made in the schedule of marginal rates. In this case, the choice is between a system relatively more progressive for large families (the exemption route) and one relatively more progressive for small families and single individuals (the credit route). The issue is one of distribution of tax burden *within* income classes among families of different sizes. By varying the rate structures we could assure that, for example, families with three members observe the same progressivity of burden with income under either the credit or exemption. We would then find that at the upper end of the income distribution families of four or more members bear more of the burden under the credit system than with exemptions, and at the lower end of the income distribution larger families are burdened more by exemptions than by credits. Which pattern would better serve the cause of equity is debatable, and I can see no clear basis for the presumption that makes tax credits "the most fundamental change" in the tax package.

An interesting effect of the credit, which seems not to have received much attention, is the change in the marginal rate applicable to the first dollar of taxable income. Under the credit system, the point at which income becomes taxable depends upon the lower-rate brackets: you don't pay any tax until you accumulate enough precredit liability. The tax-exempt income level will be $11,884 for a couple with four children under the Carter proposal, for example, bringing the family into the tax system in the 19 percent marginal rate bracket. A married couple with no children reaches the taxable level at $6,553 under the Carter proposal, with a marginal rate of 17 percent. Reductions in the lower-bracket rates would just push the tax-exempt income level higher, dropping to zero the marginal rate of the barely taxable family and raising the marginal rate at which families enter the positive tax zone. Similarly, changes in the rate of credit do *not* change *marginal* rates, except for taxpayers whose liability is reduced to zero. For them the effect is to reduce the marginal rate to zero.

As far as the overall progressivity of the individual income tax system is concerned, the proposed changes appear to be rather progressive. For a four-person, one-earner family, for example, with only earned income, the income tax changes range from a cut of 70 percent at the $10,000 level to a cut of 12 percent at the $20,000 level, to an increase of 2 percent at the $100,000 level. A number of the detailed changes in the individual tax will have the effect of including in the tax base a greater fraction of the returns to saving, and this will also increase the progressivity of the tax with respect to income.

Another element to be considered is the social security payroll tax. For a one-earner family of four, the recently enacted changes in the FICA tax when combined with the Carter proposals result in a reduction in the sum of the two taxes from $1,616 to $1,360, a cut of 16 percent, not 70 percent. At the $20,000 level there is an increase of 6 percent, from $4,110 to $4,362, instead of a reduction of 12 percent; while at the $100,000 level the increase is 5 percent instead of 2 percent. In all of these figures I have regarded both the employee and employer share of the FICA taxes as borne by the worker, surely not the perfect way to describe the matter, but probably better than the assumption that only the employee's share is borne by him.

These figures illustrate the apparent increase in burden on the middle-income taxpayer that results when the FICA taxes are taken into account. For the two-earner families the situation would be somewhat different and would depend on the division of earnings between the spouses, since much of the tax increase results from raising the ceiling on covered earnings. But for a two-earner family with combined earnings around $40,000, the result would again be a rather hefty increase in taxes.

Whether we should *really* regard this as an increase in burden is an interesting issue. It has always been recognized that tax revenues would be needed to maintain the social security system. The accumulating unfunded liabilities were presumably expected to be met by taxes paid by *someone*. Since there were few solutions with a serious political chance of being approved, perhaps one should say that the FICA tax increases took place when the social security benefit structure was enacted.

On the subject of progressivity, two further points should not be neglected. The first concerns the need to take into account inflation, which has the effect of narrowing the marginal rate brackets in real terms and pushing families with given real incomes higher into the rate schedule. Since the Treasury data show an increase in progressivity in nominal terms, attributable to the Carter proposals, we may conclude that the natural progressivity-increasing effect of inflation is being reinforced. Added to this is the tendency for inflation to work through the rules of income measurement to increase the nominal return to capital relative to the real return. This also tends to increase the progressivity of the tax system, since it raises the effective tax on capital income, which is relatively concentrated among high-bracket taxpayers.

The second point concerns the relationship between the corporation and individual income taxes. The Treasury analysis concludes that when the corporate rate cuts are taken into account the average rate of taxation of capital income is reduced by the Carter proposal. Whatever one may make of the precise figures, it is likely that the corporate rate cut tends, perhaps significantly, to reduce the progressivity (with respect to income) of the combined tax system.

Income Measurement and Tax Expenditure Issues

The reform elements of the President's 1978 tax program fall into two broad groups: (1) those designed to bring about a closer correspondence between the effective tax base and the income concept known in technical jargon as Haig-Simons income;[2] and (2) those designed to alter programs that subsidize certain activities, which I shall call the tax expenditure programs. Those measures intended to broaden the tax base can in turn be grouped into those seeking to redefine or broaden the definition of consumption, those with the effect of bringing a large fraction of saving into the base and those having both effects at once. Under the Haig-Simons definition, income is conceived of as the sum of consumption and savings. Naturally, some proposals fit more than one of these classes; some fit none too well. Table 2 lists the individual measures, together with their 1979 calendar year liability effects, by this loose classification. Liability effects for individuals and corporations are lumped together since the same analysis applies basically to both.

Broaden the Definition of Consumption. In the class of proposals to broaden the concept of consumption in the tax base are two of some significance for both revenue and the policy issues concerned. Repealing the deductions for state and local gasoline, general sales, and miscellaneous taxes is estimated to raise calendar 1979 liability by nearly $4 billion. Repealing these deductions is frequently advocated as an improvement in the measurement of income, the argument being that these taxes are simply part of household expenditure. To the extent that there are systematic differences in price levels among jurisdictions as a consequence of different rates of tax, there is a case for keeping the deductions as a device for income measurement. Since these deductions tend to be made by a rule of thumb rather than according to actual expense records, and since variation across states is fairly limited, the main effect of this change would be to shift the burden from nonitemizers to itemizers and, within the latter group, to simplify the tax system.

TABLE 2

A Classification of the Carter Reform Proposals

Proposals	Liability Effect, Calendar Year 1979 (millions of dollars)
Broaden the Definition of Consumption	
Repeal deductions for gasoline, sales, and miscellaneous taxes	3,908
Limit employer deduction for business entertainment and meals	1,476
More Fully Tax Returns to Savings	
Repeal capital gains alternate tax	140
Tax interest earnings in annuity contracts on accrual	12
Repeal deduction of half regular tax for minimum tax	284
Require straight-line depreciation and longer lives for buildings	101
Require corporate family farms to use accrual accounting	40
Make bad-debt reserves more realistic	286
Phase out DISC over three years	664
Phase out deferral of tax on foreign subsidiaries	88
Make Other Changes in the Direction of Haig-Simons Income	
Substitute combined medical and casualty expense	1,909
Tax unemployment benefits for higher income taxpayers	212
Tax employee death benefits	32
Extend "at risk" rule to individuals and corporations	14
Change Certain Tax Expenditure Programs	
Introduce state and local taxable bond option	182
Introduce nondiscrimination rule for health and group term life plans	32
Repeal political contributions deduction	2
Extend and restructure investment tax credit	−2,366
Change Credits, Exemptions and Rates	
Give $240 credit and reduce individual tax rates	−23,538
Reduce corporate tax rate	−5,965
Total all income tax proposals	−22,487

Eliminating the employer deductions for much business entertainment and limiting the deduction for business meals to half the outlay is a change that might appear to raise the taxes on business, but it is explicitly intended to raise the taxes on people—the employees now receiving the associated benefits of consumption. Just as it makes no difference for the incidence or allocation effects (after adjustment) whether a tax is levied on the supplier or the demander of a good, it doesn't matter whether the expenditure is disallowed as a deduction for the employer or considered as income of the employee, as long as the rates of tax are the same. That rates of tax are not the same has some effect on the analysis, as will be discussed below.

This reform is generally regarded as serving the interests of horizontal equity—some people pay for their own lunches out of after-tax dollars, while others get their lunches tax free because their employers pay for them. This view fails to take account of the process of competition in labor markets which determines employee compensation and which tends to equalize the net-of-tax reward received by individuals of similar ability. When rules have been in place for some time, tax-free consumption will have become a determinant of the pecuniary compensation structure, much as the nonpecuniary advantages of academic life seem to be reflected in university salaries. Under these circumstances a *change* in the rules is likely to introduce temporary inequities, upsetting the equivalence of after-tax treatment previously established.

There is a concern for vertical equity in this case as well. By and large it seems to be taken for granted that the recipients of the tax-free consumption are well-to-do. No doubt the circumstances of these employees in fact vary considerably, but in a progressive system there is an obvious pressure from high-bracket (and hence well-to-do) employees for nontax advantages. We should expect to find a larger share of lightly taxed forms of income among high-bracket taxpayers than among low-bracket taxpayers. While it is somewhat difficult to make this precise, we may guess that the fraction of income that is tax exempt rises on average with the marginal tax rate applicable. Whether the result is vertical inequity depends upon how progressive we want the tax to be with respect to real income.

Ironically, the proposed treatment of business entertainment and meals is less than ideal from the point of view of vertical equity. For obvious administrative reasons it limits the employer deduction instead of requiring employees to include this consumption as income. Thus the transaction is taxed at the employer's marginal tax rate, typically the corporate rate, and does not vary with the circumstances of the individual taxpayer.

Thus it is mainly by reducing the overall amount of tax-exempt consumption, not its distribution, that the effect will be felt. This influence on the equilibrium quantity of entertainment and restaurant meals is the strongest basis for the new rules. Since these forms of compensation are tax-favored, they probably play a disproportionately large role in market equilibrium. A good presumption is that the proposed treatment will tend to improve resource allocation by leading to a redistribution of the consumption of restaurant meals and entertainment and smaller amounts of both. Naturally there is concern about the latter on the part of producers of restaurant and entertainment services, a concern that might reasonably be met by phasing in the changes instead of introducing them all at once.

More Fully Tax Returns to Savings. The proposals under the heading "More Fully Tax Returns to Savings" vary in their approaches and also in the extent to which they might better be regarded as improving the allocation of whatever saving takes place. Repealing the alternative tax on capital gains and taxing the accruing interest on annuity contracts simply increase the fraction of the yield from savings in the tax base. The same may be said of the tightening up of the minimum tax, which translates basically into an increase in the tax on capital gains. Reforming depreciation allowances for real estate, requiring accrual accounting for corporate family farms, making bad-debt reserves more realistic, phasing out DISC, phasing out deferral of tax on the retained earnings of controlled foreign corporations—all increase the amount of capital income in the tax base, but by reducing the favored treatment of certain lines of investment they are also directed at efficiency gains.

The effort to make more consistent the tax treatment of the returns to various forms of real assets (such as equipment and structures) seems likely to improve the allocation of investment resources and is to be applauded. As one inclined to support consumption-based taxes, on grounds primarily of equity but also of efficiency, I am less persuaded of the merits of such obvious reforms as repeal of the alternative tax on capital gains, tightening of the minimum tax, and taxation of accruing interest in retirement annuities. But if Haig-Simons income is the desired base, these reforms make sense.

Other Changes in the Direction of Haig-Simons Income. In the third section of Table 2 are miscellaneous proposals which generally make taxable income conform more closely to a consistent Haig-Simons definition. The major effects on revenue and redistribution would stem from combining medical and casualty loss deductions and subjecting them to a much higher nondeductible floor than at present, to constitute one "extraordinary expense" deduction. The idea behind these deductions is that, beyond some reasonable level, outlays for medical services constitute neither consumption nor saving and hence are not part of income, while a casualty loss does represent a reduction in wealth and hence dissaving over the accounting period, unmatched by an increase in consumption.

Both these deductions have always had peculiar features regarded purely as income measurement devices. The casualty loss deduction in particular is anomalous since other losses of nonbusiness wealth (depreciation of household capital, for example) are not taken into account in calculating taxable income, nor is the value of services generated by such assets.

In support of the proposed reform, the administration stresses that deductions for these expenses constitute a kind of catastrophe insurance and, in the administration's view, now offer an unnecessary amount of insurance, especially to high-bracket taxpayers. There is a risk in singling out the insurance aspect of these particular deductions. Even under the administration's proposal the anomaly remains that the government pays a higher fraction of covered expenses for a higher-bracket taxpayer. One may ask why not go all the way and offer a flat coinsurance rate (a refundable tax credit) instead of a varying rate (via the deduction)?

The answer indicates why this proposal is in the income measurement and not the tax expenditure section of Table 2. In the perennial rediscovery that deductions are "worth" more to high-bracket than to low-bracket taxpayers it seems often to be overlooked that, if taxpaying capacity is measured by ex post results, an income tax is inherently a sort of insurance system. It absorbs part of gains and shares part of losses. Naturally, in a progressive system, the government bears a fraction of the losses that is larger for those in high brackets than that for low-bracket taxpayers. The administration is thus arguing that consumption in Haig-Simons income includes ordinary outlays for the classes of expenditures called medical expenses and casualty losses, but not "extraordinary" outlays, and the insurance consequences follow directly from this.

Because an ex post income tax functions inherently as an insurance program, it encourages self-insurance. Tucked into the administration's medical expense proposal is the very important suggestion that the deduction of half of medical insurance premiums, independently of floor, be discontinued. This feature of the present law can be regarded as offsetting the encouragement of self-insurance—it gives a sort of break to those who cannot take advantage of the medical deduction

38

that covers only uninsured outlays. (Another method would be to ignore insurance in computing the deduction.) While it is commonly said that public policy should encourage individuals to purchase insurance (and the administration takes this position with respect to employer-provided health insurance), a significant counter-argument is that self-insured individuals have a greater incentive to seek out the most economical form of care.

The recommendation that unemployment benefits be included in the tax base sets an important precedent. The advantages of promoting horizontal equity and eliminating anomalies by which the tax advantages may substantially increase the attractiveness of being unemployed seem very persuasive. Before unemployment benefits are included in the base, however, income must reach a regrettably high level ($20,000 for a single taxpayer, $25,000 for a couple), and it is hoped that this sort of income test is not the real precedent in the proposal.

One aspect which seems to have received little attention is how the inclusion of unemployment benefits will affect the effective marginal tax rates for non-unemployment benefit income. Since each dollar of income above the threshold results in the inclusion of another half dollar of unemployment benefits in the tax base, the marginal rates on the other income are thereby also increased by 50 percent.

The extension of the "at risk" rule (limiting deductions with respect to certain investments financed by nonrecourse loans) to individuals and corporations carries further a device inaugurated in the Tax Reform Act of 1976 to offset glaring inadequacies in other income measurement rules with respect to certain assets (such as phonograph records) and certain forms of transactions (such as installment sales). These inadequacies allow the manufacture of deductions to which no income corresponds. Consequently, transactions of great artificiality are induced with the only effect being tax reduction. "At risk" seems to be an attempt to restrict this practice directly, an alternative to repairing the basic rules. The new restrictions will not be applied to real estate investment. Treasury explains that this is because nonrecourse financing is used legitimately in this area; a better explanation of what is "legitimate" would perhaps suggest a less complex correction.

Change Certain Tax Expenditure Programs. Proposals to provide a subsidy to the issue of taxable state and local bonds have two principal objectives: (1) to increase the transfer to these local governments per unit of federal cost, either in direct outlays or in the form of forgone tax receipts, and (2) to increase the progressivity of the income tax. The latter occurs if the subsidy percentage is set higher than the prevailing discount of tax-exempt from fully taxable interest. This discount, in recent years roughly 30 percent, in effect puts a ceiling on the rate of tax on interest from comparable financial assets. If the discount is stepped up to 40 percent, tax collections will be increased as taxpayers in the 30 to 40 percent brackets switch to taxable bonds. Hence the positive liability effect of this proposal; there is in addition an ordinary outlay on the other side of the budget that exceeds this revenue pick-up. This is a second best treatment of these transactions—though perhaps the best attainable politically. It does move the subsidy in the direction of a normal outlay program, but at the cost of increasing the already excessive incentive for state and local government borrowing.

Of minor revenue significance are the proposed nondiscrimination requirements for employer-provided health and group term life insurance plans, and of no estimated revenue significance are the new requirements with respect to integration of social security with qualified retirement plans. But both proposals raise important issues of tax policy. These rules are designed to ensure that these fringe benefits enjoying tax preference are sufficiently widely shared by obliging employers to provide their low-bracket employees benefits in relation to those provided to high-bracket employees and owners. My guess about what has happened is that once minor deviations from good Haig-Simons income measurement—in effect items that the average person doesn't regard as "income"—have become enshrined in law, those who would reform the rules are required to find a way to live with the anomalies. Hence, one must find a policy interest in the provision by employers of compensation to their employees in the form of retirement benefits, medical insurance, disability insurance, life insurance, and the like. Once this is conceded one has to discover the particular people for whom these benefits are really intended (the rank and file) and design the rules in such a way that the rascals for whom they are not intended (the high-bracket management) at least share with others.

In arguing for the proposed rule changes, the administration fails to ask why employers would resist providing the benefits in question if the employees preferred them to cash wages. Consider, for example, retirement benefits. If we ask why an employer would offer a retirement plan to his employees in the absence of an income tax or similar levy, it seems clear that the principal reason would be economy of administration and the like. Naturally, since an income tax raises the price of future consumption, if it can be avoided through a retirement plan provided by employers there will be a distinct incentive for individuals to seek to have their compensation in that form. This incentive is most strongly felt by employees for whom the marginal tax rate is high, and a little experimentation with the phenomenon of compound interest will confirm the reasons for this relationship. That the rank and file don't bargain harder for this form of compensation could be predicted by economic theory; they would be expected to prefer cash that they can spend as they wish, and the tax advantages of saving in this form are lower for them. (As they are driven into higher marginal rate brackets one would expect this to change as well except insofar as social security more than keeps up.)

If we really want an income base, shouldn't we include all contributions and earnings in the base of each employee? If we also want to urge people to participate in retirement pension plans, does it make any sense in a progressive tax system to exclude retirement contributions and earnings on them from income as the basis for this subsidy? My guess is that we backed into the present treatment of retirement pensions because of the general concept of income as a cash flow, and I would note again the case to be made for adopting that view. Stopping halfway to a consumption base has given us such features of the tax law as requirements for qualification of retirement plans for tax preference. Now some new nondiscrimination rules to force employers to pay a "tax" in the form of compensation for the rank and file, which they value at less than the cost to the employer, so that upper-bracket management can get the tax advantage on retirement savings for themselves.

Remarks of a similar kind apply to the Treasury analysis of the medical disability and life insurance nondiscrimination issue, though in this case the issue is more one of consumption measurement. Since life insurance, medical insurance, and disability insurance premiums are not deductible from income in the ordinary course of events, there is clearly no reason why they should be allowed as exclusions from income of employees. Once this exception is made, however, the exclusion is of much more interest to high-bracket employees than to the low-bracket rank and file. Instead of eliminating the exclusion, the Treasury's proposals would force the high-bracket management to compensate their low-bracket employees in the form of benefits that they value at less than the cost, in order that management can get some tax subsidies. Isn't this a place to apply the tax expenditure point of view and get these programs out of the tax system?

Since the taxation of business is discussed elsewhere, I shall make only two comments on the restructuring and extension of the investment tax credit. The first is to note the irony of striving to increase the income progressivity of the tax system, and in particular to raise the tax on the return to capital, while at the same time increasing the subsidy to capital formation via the investment tax credit. The second is to regret that the administration was not more ambitious. Here again the appeal of a straight expenditure approach is very strong. Enormous mischief has resulted from running this subsidy program through the tax system. Who would think of obliging a farmer to have tax liability to qualify for a subsidy? Who would consider not including the farmer's receipts under the subsidy program in his income calculation? Is it not unfortunate that the investment stimulus program was not thought through in these terms at its inception?

Conclusion

Overall the administration's tax program appears to move in the direction of a more coherent and consistent income tax base—an issue separate from the progressivity of the tax on that base. Obviously a great many issues have been raised and dealt with thoughtfully; it is not a lightweight package as some have suggested. On the other hand, the program is modest by comparison with that implied by the Treasury option papers leaked to the press last fall. Someone has described what remains as "everything but the main course."

The dishes that have been omitted from the banquet this time are sure to be ordered again. Prominent among them is rationalization of the way income generated by corporations is taxed—that is, integration of the corporate and individual income tax. The administration trial balloon would have combined a rather well-thought-through integration plan with full taxation of capital gains and a substantial reduction in the individual rates, to a top rate of 50 percent. That plan would certainly have been a main course worth lingering over.

Also missing from the present menu, but offered in the earlier one, is attention to the penalty on two-earner married couples. This is a matter of equity, essentially involving the tax-free nature of income within the household, but also an important matter of efficiency. While econometric evidence leaves open to doubt the elasticity of the labor supply to changes in wages for primary workers (and no one has attempted to measure the effects of wages on such factors as the *quality* of labor supplied or the choice of careers), there is a lot of evidence that among secondary workers the labor supply is rather responsive to the after-tax wage. This is a happy case when arguments of equity and of efficiency seem to work together. The corrective actions—some sort of credit or exemption with respect to the earnings of secondary workers—do not seem difficult to implement, and it seems both right and likely that something will be done along these lines in the longer run.

Another glaring omission from this tax program, as in the earlier option papers, is any concern for the effects of inflation. As mentioned earlier, inflation alters real tax burdens by narrowing brackets in real terms and pushing people into higher rates, an effect that is easily corrected by congressional action. More serious is the effect on income measurement. For example, the Treasury in 1976 estimated that if the measuring rod for depreciation allowances were changed from historical cost to current dollars, corporate tax liability would have been reduced by $6 billion. And many people have experienced some frustration at paying taxes on interest earnings that were insufficient to hold savings account balances constant in real terms. This is not the place to commence serious discussion of the issues involved, but these examples suggest that shortcomings in the tax system during times of inflation will demand attention in the future.

I mentioned earlier that changes in the treatment of second workers in married couples had strong appeal on grounds of both equity and efficiency; another idea that was omitted from the administration's program also has considerable appeal on both grounds. This is the view that a shift from a Haig-Simons income to a consumption base tax would rationalize much that we already do (such as tax-deferred retirement savings, subsidized investment via investment tax credit, accelerated depreciation, taxation of capital gains on realization basis). Such a shift would greatly simplify many of the most complex areas of the tax law (corporate integration, tax shelters, capital gains), correct a bias toward early consumers and late earners that is without any discernible ethical or social merit, and probably lead to a substantially more efficient allocation of resources.

From the perspective of these big issues the reform of 1978 may appear somewhat tame. But given the apparent lack of political interest in changing the tax laws, modesty on the part of the administration is understandable. A poll not too long ago found the respondents heavily in favor of tax reform, but very few people thought it was a good idea to restrict the property tax deduction or the mortgage interest deduction or the gasoline tax deduction. I don't know what they thought about requiring the inclusion of accruing interest on retirement annuities, but I would guess that anyone who knew what it was would be against that idea too. Senator Long is probably right when he says that tax reform means "Don't tax you, don't tax me, tax the fellow behind the tree."

NOTES

[1] *Report of the Council of Economic Advisers,* January 1978, p. 216; emphasis added.

[2] For an explanation of this concept see, for example, U.S. Treasury Department, *Blueprints for Basic Tax Reform,* January 17, 1977, chapter 2.

Summary of Discussion

The discussion opened with a number of questions regarding the distributional impact of the President's tax proposals when it is adjusted for the effects of inflation and the 1977 changes in social security legislation. Sunley's Table 8 showed that the combined burden of employees' social security taxes and income taxes would rise between 1977 and 1979 on four-person, one-earner families earning real incomes above about $17,000 measured in 1977 dollars, while the combined burden would fall on income below this level. John Hamm said that he had carried the computation out to 1980, and one extra year's inflation and social security tax changes lowered the break-even point to $12,500. Sunley did not doubt this estimate, but suggested that further tax cuts might be introduced by 1980.

Michael Boskin said that Sunley's table should assume that employees were also burdened by the employer's share of the social security tax. Attiat Ott went further, suggesting that burden tables should also show changes in the burden resulting from deficit financing and corporate tax changes. Bradford agreed in principle, but said that we did not have the knowledge to distribute such burdens.

Sunley also agreed in principle, but noted that it was very difficult to change the way in which burden tables were presented to the Congress. This year the Treasury used an expanded income concept in its tables for the first time in place of adjusted gross income, and even this minor change had provoked the charge that the Treasury was trying to hide something. Sunley suggested that it was necessary to educate the Congress and the general public a great deal more before it would be possible to make further significant changes in burden tables.

Peggy Musgrave asked whether the Treasury had considered some sort of refundable tax credit to aid those low-income individuals and families who paid no taxes. Sunley noted that the President's welfare program expanded the earned income credit and suggested that the tax-writing committees may be examining the earned income credit in this round of tax cutting and tax reform.

Richard Musgrave pointed out that the Haig-Simons definition of income or accretion referred to consumption plus saving, while Bradford's Table 2 analyzed the impact of the President's program on the consumption base and on the return to saving rather than on the total income (consumption plus saving) base. Musgrave warned that preoccupation with measures to broaden the consumption component of the base could lead to disregard of the equally important need for fuller inclusion of the savings component. The net result could well be to damage the chances of full-base oriented income tax reform. If a move was to be made in the direction of a consumption tax, it should take the form of replacing part of income tax revenue with a full-fledged supplementary consumption tax. But this should not interfere with broadening the income tax base across both consumption and savings components. Boskin commented that he would prefer an explicit announcement that a consumption tax was the ultimate goal which would then be phased in. On the other hand, he noted that the current income tax system taxes only a small part of economic income, and most tax reformers do not object to moving to a more broadly based income tax in a piecemeal fashion.

Bradford and Sunley differed over the wisdom of the administration's effort to restrict the degree to which private pension plans that are integrated with social security could discriminate in favor of highly paid employees. Bradford felt that employees should be able to bargain freely for straight wages in place of pension plans. Sunley noted that the Treasury plan was primarily aimed at small, closely held corporations where the top management exploited the tax system's favorable treatment of pensions while providing little or no pension protection for their employees.

Jude Wanniski expressed his dismay that neither paper critically examined the progressivity of the income tax system. In his view, many of the loopholes in the system were a response to the progressivity of its marginal rates. Sunley replied that it was a chicken-or-egg problem. The loopholes may be a response to the progressive rates or vice versa. He stated that it was the administration's long-run goal to broaden the tax base so that marginal rates could be lowered. Bradford said that he had attempted to keep his paper neutral with respect to matters concerning the distribution of the tax burden, but that he personally favored a tax system that would use consumption as a base and would tax that base progressively, perhaps in a more progressive manner than at present.

PART THREE

BUSINESS TAXES

Taxation and Capital Formation: Missing Elements in the President's Tax Program

Michael J. Boskin and *Jerry Green*

The most important problem facing the U.S. economy today is the insufficient rate of capital formation. This is not merely a short-run problem tied to the current recovery and recent inflation. The grossly inadequate saving rate is fundamental and pervasive, involving an enormous waste of resources. The social rate of return to saving exceeds the private rate because of the extremely heavy taxation of capital income. National income in the future could be increased dramatically by a relatively mild reduction in current consumption, thereby channeling output into capital formation.

The need for an increase in the rate of capital formation is now widely recognized by professional economists. In the short run, increased investment may help sustain the recovery and expand employment; in the long run, increased saving is needed to help meet the impending retirement income needs of the baby-boom generation. By the year 2025 the ratio of retirees to workers will increase by almost 70 percent, and the projected deficit in the social security system will reach crisis proportions.[1] One way to ameliorate this problem is to rely more heavily on private saving to finance retirement consumption, which would entail an increase in capital formation during the intervening years.

The need for capital formation has also been recognized in a variety of recent tax reform recommendations. Unfortunately, although few issues stir as much controversy as does tax reform, there is much misunderstanding of the U.S. tax system and its economic effects. Nowhere is this confusion more evident than in the discussion of tax reform to stimulate capital formation. Indeed, while virtually everyone favors tax reform, there are at least three different definitions of it in popular discussions. First, tax reform can mean a balanced reduction in taxes and government expenditures, that is, a reduced size of the public sector. This is the sense in which former President Ford discussed tax reform in the last election campaign. As indicated below, changes in the share of income accruing to the public sector can have a substantial impact on private saving and also on national capital formation—whether they reflect the large automatic nominal income elasticity of tax revenues or are induced by discretionary tax policies.

Second, tax reform can mean changing specific features of various taxes, for example, dividend relief for partial integration of corporate and personal income

---

The views in this paper are our own and not necessarily those of the officers or trustees of the National Bureau of Economic Research.

taxes or changes in the investment tax credit. President Carter usually uses the term in this sense, and it appears to be the method by which he hopes his policies will induce capital formation.

Third, tax reform can mean changing the composition of a given tax revenue among different tax bases, for example, shifting some social security programs from payroll tax to general revenue finance. Approximately one year ago, in its *Blueprints for Basic Tax Reform,* the Treasury Department outlined in great detail the program favored by most economists to stimulate capital formation: ending the double taxation of saving by switching the base of personal taxation from income to consumption—is potentially an extremely effective vehicle.

Failure to distinguish among these three types of tax reform and to trace carefully through their combined economic effects on capital formation is a source of continued confusion. We are afraid that the general public discussion of the President's tax program is no exception. Various parts of the program, such as the investment tax credit and the cut in corporate tax rates, have often been singled out for discussion; others, including the automatic tendency of tax revenues to rise more rapidly than income (and hence decrease private income and saving) and the enormous legislated increases in social security taxes, have not received adequate attention in the discussion of the *net* impact of these combined tax policies on capital formation.

The purpose of this exposition is to analyze the likely effects of the President's tax policies on capital formation. Toward this end, we first analyze the likely effects on capital markets of the President's major business tax proposals. Proposals such as the decrease in the corporate tax rate and the extension of the investment tax credit, while highly desirable to promote the efficient use of the capital stock, are judged extremely unlikely to have more than a negligible impact on capital formation. The explanation lies in a basic, yet often overlooked fact: Policies which increase the demand for investment have not been combined with policies to increase private saving, that is, the supply of new capital. Just as stimulating the demand for any commodity in inelastic supply will tend primarily to bid up its price, so these policies will most likely merely increase interest rates. If private income, after taxes, was not affected by the combined tax policies, the modest positive interest elasticity of private saving would produce a small increase in saving and hence capital formation.[2] Unfortunately, the President's policy is almost certain to reduce private income and saving substantially.

In the section on "Overall Effects on Capital Formation" we discuss the combined effects of the President's 1978 tax proposals, the legislated social security tax increases, and the propensity of the tax revenue system to take ever larger shares of private income in the course of real economic growth and especially inflation. Our conclusion is that the net impact on capital formation is likely to be a worsening of the long-run capital shortage, and we find these proposals devoid of a serious attempt to address this problem. We also point out some other potential problems and inconsistencies in the relationship between the announced goals of the tax reforms and their likely economic effects.

The paper concludes with a brief summary and suggestions of potential policies to deal with the problem of long-run capital formation.

48

Corporate Tax Changes and Capital Formation

Changes in the structure of corporate taxation primarily affect the demand for investment. An analysis of the implications for capital formation must involve the interaction of both sides of the capital market. In this section we will trace only a piece of the picture. But because of the close connections among corporate decisions, household savings behavior, and government budget constraints, we will necessarily venture a bit beyond the corporate walls on occasion.

Productive capital of corporations is the most important form of fixed investment and the one most directly sensitive to tax policy. Privately held capital, housing stock in particular, responds to cost conditions, but it is not the subject of the present tax proposals in any important respect. Government saving is an increasingly important component of capital formation, and we shall argue below that the present tax changes may have substantial, negative, indirect effects on it at the state and local level. Our analysis will focus primarily on the market for corporate financing decisions, however, and will trace the effects through the major sectors of the economy.

Retained earnings and issues of debt are the two principal instruments of corporate financial policy. New equity is quantitatively minor and, with today's historically low equity values, does not really provide much of a margin for the corporate sector as a whole. The corporate income tax and the investment tax credit influence the costs of these two main sources of capital and change the relative prices of capital and labor as well. An analysis of the effects on capital formation of the corporate income tax and the investment tax credit must therefore treat the question of the supply elasticities for all factors, and it must be explicit about the time frame considered and the process by which price and income expectations are formulated. Needless to say, a full study of these questions is beyond the scope of this short paper, but we hope to raise the central issues and to shed some light on them.

The Net Marginal Product of Capital, the Cost of Capital, and the Demand for Investment. There are conflicting schools of thought regarding the neutrality of the corporate income tax with respect to the choice of capital intensity in the corporate sector. Those who believe that new investment is financed on the margin entirely by debt argue for neutrality, because interest on debt is deductible for tax purposes. The net cost of capital would be unchanged. Others contend that with equity finance the reduction in the corporate tax rate would clearly lower costs and thereby stimulate expansion. Obviously, the truth lies somewhere in between.

What is less well understood is how changes in the corporate tax rate would affect investors holding different financial assets. It is important to assess these differential effects because sustained growth can result only from an increase in savings, and the supply of savings in different forms may have rather different elasticities with respect to the rate of return. A recent study shows rather surprisingly that, even if debt and equity are both inelastically supplied, part of the change in the corporate tax is passed on to the holders of debt.[3] This contradicts the intuition that debt would be unaffected since its marginal cost is the same to the corporation.

The reason is that when the corporate rate falls, the firm wants to expand debt. For firms to be willing to issue only the amount of debt supplied by the private sector, the gross interest cost must rise. Rough calculations have indicated that interest rates on all assets can be quite sensitive to the tax structure. We would guess that, in the long run, a 3 percent decrease in the corporate tax rate could increase the net rate of return to lenders by about 0.3 percentage points. The long-run rate of return to equity should increase by about 0.2 percentage points. Thus, surprisingly, debt holders should benefit more than equity holders from a cut in the corporate tax rate despite the fact that interest is a deductible expense.

This computation is based on a long-run full-employment model in which saving is independent of the rate of return. The results are therefore to be treated with appropriate caution; nevertheless, they indicate that relatively small changes in the corporate tax will raise the rate of return by a very large fraction of its original amount.

Effects of Higher Interests Costs on Other Sectors of the Capital Market and on Capital Accumulation in the Long Run. Higher nominal interest rates will undoubtedly put pressure on the other principal borrowers in the U.S. capital markets, that is, on households and state and local governments. Higher carrying costs will also affect the size of the federal deficit but are unlikely to have any direct effect on saving at that level. It is important to remember that state and local government borrowing is about one-third the size of borrowing by nonfinancial corporations and cannot be neglected.

Although state and local budgets now show a surplus, the long-term prospects must be viewed as precarious. The majority of their revenues are precommitted, either to services or welfare, and much of this is mandated by law. Any increase in the cost of borrowing will fall quite heavily on capital spending in the long run. In the short run, postponement is always easier to justify than cancellation and is much easier than reducing jobs, so there could be a substantial cutback in capital formation within this sector if interests costs rise.

Short-Run Impacts of the Tax Changes on Investment. The short-run implications of the administration's proposals depend very heavily on the state of the economy at the time they are adopted and particularly on the state of expectations. If there is considerable slack in the investment goods sector, there will certainly be a spurt of capital spending. It would be a mistake, however, to attribute this entirely to reduced costs of capital. Some commitments to capital improvements may have been postponed in anticipation of these changes, so that an immediate recovery in this sector could represent catching up rather than the beginning of a trend.

By extending the investment tax credit to structures as well as equipment, the administration has taken a logical step toward simplification of the tax code and the removal of artificial distortions. The extent to which capital accumulation can take this form depends on the competition between residential and business construction within the highly cyclical construction industry.

The nature of the short-run adjustment depends on the assumptions made about the rigidity of prices. With prices fixed, a general expansion due to lower unit costs would increase the demand for both capital and labor. But if prices are primarily cost determined and are relatively flexible (or are free to increase at a slower rate in nominal terms in a generally inflationary period), then the investment tax credit and reduction in the corporate rate will produce a movement along the factor-price frontier. This is the short-run analogue of the long-run change in the components of the cost of capital discussed above. Factors exist in fixed quantities and, for the short run at least, are inelastically supplied. Decreases in the price of capital services in relation to that of labor must be absorbed in a lower real wage as well as a higher return to capital.

Conflicting aspects to these forces are hard to sort out in our dynamic economy because of their complex interactions with monetary forces. Less pressure for wage increases may improve the prospects for controlling inflation. If anticipated, this reduced pressure could lower nominal interest rates and might even offset the competitive forces in the capital markets driving up nominal interest rates. That is, the real net rate of return could rise without a change in the nominal rate.

But this highly aggregative view of the economy may well be misleading. Labor supply may be fixed in aggregate, but different elasticities of substitution in various sectors will mean that wage rates would have to change differentially in order to maintain the current sectoral levels of employment. This would set up further frictional forces that would decrease employment overall as the economy adjusts to new relative factor prices in the short run. Therefore, there may be some contraction in income growth as the corporate sector shifts toward capital and away from labor, even under conditions of flexible factor prices and fixed aggregate factor supplies.

Another factor in the substitution of capital for labor is the employers' contribution to social security taxes, which is scheduled to increase dramatically under the administration's plan. Especially if the employment relationship is viewed as a long-term contract, the perception of these higher taxes in the future may dampen the employers' willingness to expand even in the present. Given the age structure of the population, many new workers will be entering the labor market, and their prospects, especially, may be hurt by these anticipations. Since saving is primarily income determined, each of these forces will affect capital accumulation in the short run as well.

Dynamics of Capital Accumulation in the Longer Run. To promote increased growth of the capital stock in the long run, any policy must generate increased savings. Despite the fact that recent research has indicated a significant positive interest elasticity of saving, the long-run effects of the currently proposed changes in the corporate tax structure will probably be small since they do not provide for dividend relief or decreased taxes on interest income at the personal level. In addition, wealth effects introduce some complicating factors. If interest rates rise, the nominal value of debt falls. For corporate debt, this fall is offset by an increase in the value of the firm, but for government debt at both the federal and lower levels the real value of perceived wealth will fall. Although this point can be attacked by the need to increase expectations of future taxes, the net effect will still be negative because some of the taxes will be borne by future generations. The holders of debt and the average taxpayer may have differential marginal propensities to save that would have a further complicating effect. On the whole, saving out of a given level of current income would increase and would serve to reinforce the original effect of higher interest rates.

But income is not logically prior to consumption, and the wealth effect may depress both income and consumption unless suitable expansionary policies are followed.

Overall Effects on Capital Formation

We have just noted that the decrease in the relative cost of equity capital implicit in the President's tax proposals is unlikely to have a large effect on capital formation unless it is accompanied by policies to expand private saving. Unfortunately, various factors suggest that the net effect of these proposals would be a substantial increase in tax revenues, not the tax cut one sees when viewing the President's 1978 proposals in isolation. These factors include the automatic increase in the share of total income accruing to the public sector because of the large income elasticity of tax revenues [4] and the enormous legislated increase in social security payroll taxes.

The President's proposed $25 billion tax cut barely offsets the automatic tax increase that will occur as nominal incomes grow and taxpayers move into higher and higher tax brackets. That is, the alleged tax cut is little more than a delayed compensation for the automatic growth in the share of income accruing to the public sector.

Worse yet, a series of social security payroll tax increases is scheduled to raise tax rates steadily over the next few years. There has been much confusion on this crucial point. The increases have been widely interpreted as amounting to $227 billion over the next decade, but this figure refers only to the estimated *additional* tax revenues due to the 1977 amendments and ignores the *previously* legislated large increases in tax rates and taxable wage base already taking effect. For example, before the 1977 amendments the rates for combined employee-employer contributions to OASDHI (old-age, survivors, disability, and health insurance) were scheduled to increase from 11.7 percent of taxable wages in 1977 to 12.1 percent in 1978–1980 and 12.6 percent in 1981. The amendments raised these rates to 12.26 percent in 1979–80 and 13.3 percent in 1981. Correspondingly, the taxable wage base was scheduled to rise from $16,500 in 1977 to $21,900 in 1981; the amendments increased the latter figure to $29,700. Thus the $227 billion figure is a substantial *underestimate* of the total increase in payroll tax now starting to take effect. This increase amounts to about $10 billion in 1978, $24 billion in 1979 relative to 1977, and much larger amounts thereafter.

It is very hard to escape the conclusion that both in the short run (over the next year or two) and over the long run (the coming decade) the share of private income going to federal taxes is likely to increase substantially.[5] What are the likely economic effects of this net transfer of resources from the private to the public sector? The answer depends upon several factors which we shall explore in turn.

First we must compare what the private sector would do with these revenues if they were not transferred to the public sector and what the government would do with them if they were so transferred. Many econometric studies suggest a substantial marginal propensity to save out of private disposable income—perhaps a

52

good estimate of savings would be 20 percent of disposable income. It is extremely unlikely that 20 percent of the legislated tax increases would find its way into government capital formation. Although government capital formation is certainly substantial, the historical trend points to a growing share of transfer payments in government spending; further, payroll tax revenues have been tied historically to social security benefit payments which accrue to a population group with a low propensity to save. Thus we conclude that *the net impact of the tax proposals will be to decrease saving and capital formation.* Before turning to policies to deal with this problem, two provisos should be kept in mind.

The President and his advisers appear to be counting on a large expansionary effect of the tax cut to increase national income. While some effect of this sort is possible, there are at least three reasons to be skeptical that this effect will be large enough to cause a *net* increase in saving and capital formation. First is the ultimate need to raise future taxes to finance the increased deficit caused by the 1978 personal and corporate tax cut. Some anticipation of these future tax increases may endanger any expansionary effects of the present tax cut. Second, with a substantial recovery underway and the unemployment rate hovering just above 6 percent, it is unclear whether there is enough slack in the economy to generate a large increase in real income as opposed to an increase in the inflation rate with deficit finance. The labor force now includes a much larger percentage of women and young workers who traditionally have much higher than average unemployment rates, and this change in composition has raised the aggregate full-employment unemployment rate above the traditional 4 to 4.5 percent. Finally, the legislated payroll tax increases also will act as a depressant on expansion.

The legislated payroll tax increases also cause a potential problem with respect to employment. While most economists agree that in the long run a substantial share of the employer's contribution is shifted to workers in the form of lower wages, it is likely that in the short run the payroll tax increases would drive up the unit costs of labor. This in turn would tend to induce incentives for both a substitution of capital for labor and a contraction in total output. Both these effects might decrease employment in the short run, which of course would directly contradict a primary goal of the income tax cuts.

Conclusion and Summary

In brief, we see little in the President's program to encourage more than a possibly minor and temporary increase in capital formation and employment. We are also deeply concerned about the failure to address the problems of long-run capital formation. The automatic tax increases due to nominal income growth and the very income elastic nature of federal tax revenues, together with the large legislated social security tax increases, will swamp the proposed income tax cuts. While the President's program is to be applauded for several reasons already mentioned and is certainly better than doing nothing about the other huge tax increases, much remains to be done. Genuine tax reform of all three types listed in the introduction should be given serious consideration as possibilities to stimulate capital formation.

First, inflation adjustment or indexing of income taxes is highly desirable. Although this would not accomplish an absolute simultaneous reduction of taxes and government expenditures, it would help offset the tendency of tax revenues to rise more rapidly than income and to decrease saving. Proposals recommended by many economists in this regard include inflation-adjustment of the rate brackets in the personal income tax and a depreciation allowance based on replacement cost rather than historical cost.

Second, dividend relief providing partial integration of the corporate and personal income taxes, or even complete corporate tax integration, should be reconsidered.

Finally, serious consideration should be given to switching from income to expenditure as the tax base. Saving should not be taxed twice. By increasing the net rate of return to saving, such a switch would substantially increase saving—and thus the capital-labor ratio, productivity, and future wages, consumption, and income—at very favorable terms to society.

NOTES

[1] See Michael J. Boskin, "Is Heavy Taxation of Capital Socially ‑Desirable?" unpublished mimeo., 1977

[2] See Michael J. Boskin, "Taxation, Saving and the Rate of Interest," *Journal of Political Economy* (April 1978); and Michael J. Boskin and Lawrence Lau, "Taxation and Aggregate Factor Supply: Preliminary Estimates," in U.S. Treasury, *Conference on Tax Research* (Washington, D.C., 1978).

[3] Martin Feldstein, Jerry Green, and Eytan Sheshinski, "Inflation and Taxes in a Growing Economy with Debt and Equity Finance," Harvard University Institute of Economic Research Working Paper (Cambridge, Mass., 1977).

[4] Henry A. Aaron, ed., *Inflation and the Income Tax* (Washington, D.C.: Brookings Institution, 1977).

[5] While it is not our purpose here to deal with the state and local sector, their revenues are also very nominal income elastic and will rise as a proportion of income without deliberate tax cuts on those levels.

Integrating the Income Taxes: Where Do We Stand?

Charles E. McLure, Jr.

In 1972 I wrote a report to the Treasury Department which was eventually published under the title "Integration of Personal and Corporate Income Taxes: The Missing Element in Recent Proposals for Tax Reform." [1] As the text of that article made clear, the reference in the title to integration as a missing element was more than descriptive; I was an early advocate of integration. [2] It was therefore with some satisfaction that I noted in July 1975 that the Ford administration was proposing to the Congress the complete elimination of the double taxation of dividends (sometimes also called partial integration) and in January 1977 that a proposal for complete integration of the income taxes was included in the Treasury Department's *Blueprints for Basic Tax Reform.* Given campaign statements by Jimmy Carter and work being done at the Treasury Department during 1977, culminating in the famous proposals to the White House reportedly leaked to the press in September of that year, an advocate of integration or dividend relief might reasonably have expected to see his efforts bear fruit in the President's recent tax message. And yet integration was not proposed. Without trying to second-guess the President or speculate on why integration or dividend relief was not included in his tax reform package, it may be worthwhile to indicate briefly some of the administrative difficulties and controversy surrounding this policy decision. Although in concept and basic principle, integration seems elegant and attractive, these impediments have kept it from being an idea whose time had come by January 1978. [3]

Full integration I fear, may not be administratively feasible. Dividend relief, however, may be feasible, and under certain conditions it would appear to achieve many of the objectives of integration. But even under ideal conditions it would not achieve all of those goals, and as actually implemented it is not likely to offer the apparent advantages of "integration by the backdoor," since the requisite conditions for achieving other objectives are quite unlikely to be realized. Finally, even dividend relief may not be as simple to administer as sometimes believed; in any event, it may be difficult to explain. For these reasons—although I continue to favor relief from double taxation of corporate-source equity income—the time may not yet be ripe for integration or dividend relief.

This paper is devoted to an elaboration of these admittedly cryptic remarks. In the sections that follow I first review briefly the faults of an unintegrated or "classical" system of taxing corporate-source equity income; these faults do, of

---

The views in this paper are my own and not necessarily those of the officers or trustees of the National Bureau of Economic Research.

course, constitute the case for integration. Then it is explained why the ideal remedy for the defects of a classical system—full integration—may not be adminisstratively feasible. Several forms of dividend relief, the fallback position if full integration is not feasible, are described, and it is suggested that, in a world without tax preferences, dividend relief would in many important respects approximate full integration. In a digression, several crucial differences in various approaches to dividend relief are described. I then discuss alternative ways of dealing with tax preferences and suggest the one that, for administrative reasons, is most likely to be adopted. But, as explained in the final section, if that approach to the problem of tax preferences is elected, the system has rather anomalous, and perhaps undesirable, effects on dividend payout policy. As a result, the approximation to full integration is less than—or at least different from—what it would be in a world of full integration or one of dividend relief without preferences. Although dividend relief would probably be worthwhile, the case may not be as clear-cut as its advocates would like to believe, especially in view of its administrative complexities.

The Case for Integration

The case for integration rests largely on its neutrality.[4] Whereas a classical system (that is, a system with an unintegrated corporate tax) distorts corporate debt-equity ratios, dividend payout rates, and the allocation of investment between the corporate and noncorporate sectors, an integrated system would be neutral in its effect on all these choices.

Depending as it does on the incidence of the corporate income tax, the equity case for integration is less easily stated categorically.[5] But in one simple version (based on the admittedly unrealistic assumption that the corporate tax is borne by shareholders), an unintegrated system is seen to have the following results: (1) Overtaxation is greatest at the bottom of the income scale; (2) *undertaxation* can occur at the top of the scale; but (3) in the aggregate the corporate tax adds to the overall progressivity of the tax system. Moreover, it produces the rather anomalous situation in which so-called tax-exempt organizations pay the corporate tax on earnings on corporate equities attributable to them.

The ideal remedy for such nonneutralities and inequities is, of course, to eliminate the corporate tax and tax corporate-source equity income to the shareholder, whether distributed or not, as in a partnership. Basis in shares would be adjusted whenever undistributed earnings were allocated and taxed to shareholders in order to prevent a double tax when shares are sold. Such a scheme can be called "integration."

Problems of Integration

Integration does, however, have a number of debilitating faults. The following is a short catalog of problems.

Most fundamentally, integration may not be constitutional since it involves taxation of income not actually received by shareholders (the retained earnings of corporations). Even if that objection is overcome (say, by making integration optional to the corporation), it could involve severe problems of cash flow for some shareholders. A 70 percent taxpayer might, for example, be forced to pay substantial taxes on imputed retained earnings that had been taxed at only the 48 percent corporate rate (which would become merely a withholding device).

Under a strict interpretation of the partnership rationale for integration it would be necessary to allocate various components of corporate income to shareholders so that they could receive the personal tax treatment accorded those types of income when received directly by individuals. Thus the corporation would report to each shareholder long-term capital gains, income on state and local securities, proceeds from life insurance, and so on, as well as ordinary income. In addition, it would report the excess of accelerated over straight-line depreciation (for use in calculation of liability for minimum tax on preference income) and the shareholder's prorated share of the investment tax credit and foreign tax credit. Thus every shareholder could easily have a number of forms to complete, which under present law plague only those with complicated finances and tax returns.[6]

A further source of a staggering load of paperwork is the need for basis adjustments. Even if corporate earnings are simply prorated to shareholders on the basis of the time that shares have been held during the year, the requirements for record keeping and transmitting information would overwhelm corporations, brokers, and shareholders. Experience with mutual funds does not lead to optimism that the burden could be handled satisfactorily.

Like income, losses should be passed through to shareholders. Because doing so on a day-to-day basis is unworkable, a day of record is needed. For technical reasons the first day of the year is not satisfactory, and using the last day opens the possibility of "trafficking in losses."

In a conceptually pure integration scheme the results of audits or amended returns would be reflected in the tax returns of shareholders who owned the firm's shares in the year for which the adjustment is made. Such an approach is, of course, impossible; therefore adjustments would of necessity be reflected in the year in which final liability is established.

Full integration would work best if corporate financial structures were simple, as they are required by law to be in the case of subchapter S corporations. In a world of various types of preferred stock and convertible debentures the difference between debt and ownership claims becomes blurred. It is possible that income might be attributed to owners of common stock and taxed to them, even though dividends are ultimately paid to owners of other securities. No satisfactory solution has yet been found for this problem.

The above problems are compounded by the existence of chains of corporate ownership. First, it may not even be possible to determine the income, tax credits, and so on of one member of such a chain until the determination has been made for all. Beyond that, consider the case of capital gains realized by corporation A on its holdings of the shares of corporation B. The allocation of these gains to owners of firm A's shares would depend both on the period that firm owned shares in firm B and the portion of that period during which individual shareholders owned shares in firm A. Other complications are created in other areas.

In short, full integration suffers from several characteristics which would make it difficult to administer and implement. Some of these would exist even under dividend relief. But others—namely basis adjustments, the cash-flow problem, the need to segregate items of income and tax preferences, and problems created by multiple classes of ownership or near ownership—are unique to (or more complicated under) integration. Until these difficulties are overcome it may be necessary to leave full integration on the back burner of tax reform.

Dividend Relief: The Fallback Position

Many economists who would like the United States to adopt integration would settle for relief from double taxation of dividends if integration were judged to be infeasible. Recognizing that most of the problems unique to integration result from the attempt to tax corporate retained earnings to the shareholder, they would propose that the income taxes be "integrated" only for distributed earnings. Businessmen, for their part, have never really been interested in integration and the heavier taxes on retained earnings it entails; from the start they have been interested only in dividend relief.[7] Other economists who might accept integration if it were feasible find dividend relief totally unacceptable on the ground of income distribution.

Dividend relief can be achieved in one of two basic ways, though the two approaches can be combined, as in Germany, and one can be converted into the other.[8] Perhaps the easiest form of dividend relief is the dividend-paid deduction. To the extent that the corporation is allowed a deduction for dividends paid, dividends, like interest, are taxed only to the shareholder at his personal marginal rate. This deduction, like all schemes for dividend relief, has no effect on the taxation of retained earnings, though it may alter dividend payout rates. No country currently employs this approach to dividend relief, though Germany employed a close relative, the split-rate system, until 1977 and continues to combine a split rate with the imputation approach described below. Under the split-rate approach a lower rate (zero in the extreme case) is applied to distributed corporate earnings than to retained earnings.

The more common approach to dividend relief goes under such names as the imputation method, the withholding approach, or, less elegantly, the gross-up and credit. Under this approach the corporation continues to pay tax on its entire taxable income. But the portion of the corporate tax that is attributable to income resulting in dividends is imputed to the shareholder and treated as a withholding tax (thus two of the names). The taxpayer "grosses up" his cash dividend to determine the amount of before-tax income (the gross dividend) that would have been needed to pay the cash dividend and includes this amount in income for tax purposes. Against his personal liability he takes credit for the corporate tax imputed to his dividends. This approach is employed in Canada, France, the United Kingdom, and, in combination with a split rate, in Germany. But only Germany provides complete relief from double taxation of dividends.

The two approaches to dividend relief can be combined, as in the German case, where retained corporate income is subject to a 51 percent tax, while distributed income is taxed at only 36 percent. The shareholder then takes a gross-up and credit based on the 36 percent rate.

58

Of perhaps greater interest is the way that one form of dividend relief can be converted into the other. If a corporation is allowed a deduction for dividends paid, but a withholding tax is applied to dividend payments, the economic result would be indistinguishable from that of the standard imputation approach. This suggests that differences between the two approaches may be more apparent than real.[9] But distinctions which may appear to be only cosmetic can have important implications, as discussed further in the next section. These implications have added significance since the proposals allegedly made to the White House by the Treasury Department and leaked to the press in early September of 1977 contained a plan for dividend relief much like that just described.

It is easy to see that in simple cases any one of the standard, combined, or convertible approaches just described could be used to remove completely the double taxation of dividends. Moreover, any degree of partial dividend relief could be produced. Perhaps more important, it can be argued that dividend relief would produce most of the results of full integration if, in addition, the top personal marginal tax rate were reduced to the neighborhood of the corporate rate. If this is true, then integration could be achieved by the back door, without having to face all the problems unique to integration.

Under a classical system, distributed corporate-source equity income is taxed more highly than other forms of income, including accrued retained earnings of corporations. Thus there is a significant tax incentive for retaining earnings rather than paying dividends.[10] Complete relief from double taxation of dividends would eliminate the differential relative to the taxation of other income, but it would leave intact the preferential taxation of retained earnings resulting in capital gains realized long after their accrual.[11] If, however, the top personal rate were no higher than the corporate rate, retentions would never carry a tax burden less than that applied to distributed corporate income, and the burden would ordinarily be greater. Thus there would be substantial pressure to distribute income. This pressure would be even greater than in the case of full integration, which would be neutral with regard to the dividend payout rate. Since the aggregate tax burden of the corporation and its shareholders would be minimized by paying out all income, there would probably be a strong tendency toward 100 percent payout, limited only by existing obligations to debt holders. To the extent that income was paid out, the result would be the taxation of corporate-source income at the rate applicable to personal income. This is, of course, exactly the result produced by integration.

Back-door integration would produce many of the desirable effects of integration. It would achieve the equity and efficiency objectives of subjecting all corporate-source income to the graduated personal rate structure applicable to other income—but at the cost of a reduction in the top bracket rate and the loss of progressivity it entails. Similarly, the choice between debt and equity would no longer be skewed so heavily in favor of debt finance; on the assumption of 100 percent payout, the tax system would not distort this financial decision. But the dividend payout decision would be strongly affected, as noted above. This distortion, if not mitigated by relatively automatic schemes for dividend reinvestment, or exactly offset by saving decisions of households, would result in a reduction in saving and, in turn, a reduction in social welfare. Moreover, because of differences in requirements for financing via retained earnings some interindustry distortions might result, but these are more problematic.

Differences in Approaches to Dividend Relief

As already noted, in a simple world without tax-exempt organizations and foreign shareholders the two approaches to dividend relief, the dividend-paid deduction and imputation methods, would produce identical results. But in the more complicated world in which we live the two approaches would not produce identical results and the differences are important.

Under the dividend-paid deduction or split-rate approaches the benefits of dividend relief extend automatically to all shareholders, including tax-exempt organizations and foreign shareholders. But under the imputation method the credit for corporate tax paid could be denied one or both of these groups. In Germany, for example, tax-exempt organizations and foreigners benefit from the reduced rate on distributed earnings but not from the gross-up and credit.

For tax-exempt organizations this distinction may be of little consequence, except as a political matter. After all, it would be easy to replicate the effects of an imputation approach which denied benefits to tax-exempt organizations by imposing a tax on dividends received by such organizations. But matters are not so simple in the international sphere. Imposition of a similar tax on dividends paid to foreign shareholders would run headlong into the basic principle of foreign tax conventions that countries should have mirror-image withholding rates. It is for this reason that Germany and the United Kingdom adopted their present systems, which rely heavily on the imputation approach, despite a basic preference for the split-rate system. Since it cannot be expected that there will be a nearly unanimous move to the dividend-paid deduction approach, the greater latitude the imputation system provides in dealing with foreign shareholders suggests that it must be presumed to be the method of choice for the United States.

Although it might reasonably be argued that the corporate tax is a withholding device that should result in refunds to foreigners to the extent that dividend relief is provided through the imputation approach, there has, in fact, been relatively little objection to the denial of the credit to foreign shareholders. An important reason for the international acceptability of imputation schemes in which no credits are allowed foreign shareholders may very well be the way in which they are packaged. The United Kingdom, for example, collects an "advance corporation tax" when dividends are paid. This tax could reasonably be interpreted as a withholding tax, given the general mechanics of the imputation method. In such an event there might be a strong case for refunds to foreign shareholders. But, as indicated by its name, the tax is, strictly speaking, a prepayment of the corporate rather than the personal tax. Thus, the British might argue, there is no case for treating it as a refundable withholding tax.

The United States might have problems with its tax treaties if it adopted the approach suggested by the Treasury Department to the White House. Under that plan, in which the dividend-paid deduction is combined with a withholding tax, it would appear unlikely that the withholding tax would not be refunded to tax-exempt organizations; certainly those organizations would receive refunds for any

60

withholding taxes on interest. But if tax-exempt organizations are granted credit for the withholding tax it would be difficult to argue persuasively in the international arena that foreign shareholders are not eligible for the same credit. Thus while the Treasury scheme is quite imaginative, some residual uncertainty must remain about whether our treaty partners would tolerate such a transparent deviation from mirror-image withholding, even if the transparency results primarily from the lack of cosmetic labeling characteristic of the British tax.

The Problem of Tax Preferences

Early discussions of integration and dividend relief generally neglected the existence of tax preferences.[12] Once the problems caused by preferences were recognized, there was a tendency to say that they could be treated in either of two ways: if the effective tax rate paid by the corporation were employed in calculating gross-up and credit, the benefits of preferences would be nullified; if the statutory rate were used, the benefits would be passed through to shareholders. Unfortunately, the first of these approaches is probably administratively infeasible, and the description is incomplete, in any event; the second is simply wrong.

Use of the effective rate for the calculation of the gross-up and credit is infeasible for several reasons.[13] First, the corporation would be required to calculate economic income as well as taxable income. Given the history of the definition of income for tax purposes and the variety of opinions about what that definition should be, this is not attractive. Second, the corporation would generally not know its effective rate soon enough for the shareholder to make his calculations of gross-up and credit on a timely basis. Beyond that, calculation of the gross-up and credit would not be straightforward in any year in which net corporate income did not equal distributions. If less than the full amount of income is distributed there would seem to be no problem; the tax preferences would, in effect, be prorated between dividends and retained earnings. But consider the case in which dividends exceed current income. It would not be satisfactory simply to use the effective corporate rate in the current year to calculate the gross-up and credit. It would be necessary to have stacking rules for the determination of the years' income from which dividends in excess of current income are presumed to be paid.

Because of the difficulties involved in using the effective tax rate to nullify tax preferences, an alternative approach is commonly used in Europe to achieve the same result. Under it a prepayment of corporate tax, or *précompte,* is employed to bring the effective rate of tax on distributed earnings up to the statutory rate. Then shareholders simply use the statutory rate to calculate their gross-up and credit, thereby avoiding many of the problems involved in use of the effective rate. But the need for stacking rules remains.

Use of the statutory rate to calculate the gross-up and credit (without *précompte*) does not, as sometimes thought, result in exact pass-through of corporate tax preferences to recipients of dividends. Instead exact pass-through involves adjustments to the gross-up and/or credit that depend on whether the preferences in question involve tax credits or tax deductions or exclusions (such as state and local interest).

Whether it is decided to pass preferences through to recipients of dividends or to nullify them—which may be decided differently for the various types of preferences—it is necessary to have stacking rules. If, for example, preferences are to be nullified to the extent that income is distributed, should dividends be assumed to come first from fully taxed income, first from preference income, or prorated from the two types of income? Again, in principle the answer need not be the same in all cases. Thus there are at least six alternative ways to treat each tax preference:

Preference income	*Pass-through*	*Nullify*
Stacked first	1	4
Prorated	2	5
Stacked last	3	6

The four alternatives (1, 2, 4, 5) that do not involve stacking preference income last necessitate measurement of economic income (or, what is the same, preference income); alternatives 3 and 6 do not require that measurement. Though there may be much to be said for passing preferences through, the European countries do not do so, and there would be strong political opposition to doing so in the United States. Thus it seems reasonable to believe that alternative 6 is the most relevant one for the United States, at least so far as deductible preferences are concerned.

Back-door Integration Revisited

It is now possible to reexamine the proposition that in a very simple world the basic equity and neutrality benefits of full integration would probably be approximated by the combination of complete dividend relief and a reduction of the top personal rate to the level of the corporate rate. If tax preferences are nullified to the extent that income is distributed, but stacked last, there is a substantial disincentive to pay dividends out of preference income. This disincentive would be especially strong for individual taxpayers in high marginal tax brackets and (if they are denied the benefits of dividend relief) for tax-exempt organizations. It therefore seems likely that the strong pressures to pay out all corporate earnings would be altered. But it is difficult to say whether the distortion of corporate dividend policy would be greater or less.

Due to the stack-last rules in alternative 6, many companies would be largely unaffected by the nullification of tax preferences on distributed corporate-source income. To the extent that retentions of such companies exceed preference income, the stacking rule would result in the preservation of preferences. But for companies with substantial preference income and high dividend payout ratios, such as banks and utilities, the situation would be quite different. Unless dividend rates could be reduced, dividend relief would result in the loss of the advantages of tax preferences for such firms and would discourage distribution of earnings.[14]

At least initially, dividend relief would probably not be complete. Thus even if the top personal rate were reduced to the level of the corporate rate, a tax penalty on the distribution of earnings would probably remain, aside from the effect of nullifying tax preferences. Back-door integration is, therefore, unlikely to be achieved.

Concluding Remarks

This extensive but partial catalog of problems to be encountered in any attempt at integration or dividend relief is not intended to be an indictment of those two approaches to tax reform. That there are controversial decisions to be made and administrative obstacles to be overcome does not, after all, mean that the decisions will not be made or that the obstacles cannot be surmounted. Serious American efforts to understand the decisions and their implications and to devise solutions for the administrative difficulties involved in integration and dividend relief have been underway for less than a year, and European analysis and experience is not an adequate guide to policy in this area. Already we understand integration and dividend relief, and especially the vital role played by tax preferences, far better than we did a year ago. Although it may be premature to press for integration or dividend relief right now, given the high cost of adopting defective legislation in such a complicated area, it may not be long before an American President can advance such a scheme with confidence that there will be few unpleasant surprises if it is adopted. Certainly the appeal of integration remains substantial—though it may be dampened a bit by consideration of administrative realities—and the search for workable schemes of integrating the tax systems continues to deserve high priority. It may be that serious efforts to find solutions to problems will be made only when a concrete legislative proposal is extant or expected. Residual difficulties should therefore not preclude the President or members of the Congress from proposing integration or dividend relief.

NOTES

[1] *Harvard Law Review,* vol. 88 (January 1975).

[2] Here I employ the term "integration" to refer to both dividend relief and integration, strictly defined. In subsequent sections the word integration applies to retained corporate earnings as well as to distributed earnings, whereas "dividend relief" is used to refer only to the removal or mitigation of the double taxation of dividends.

[3] The following fable may characterize the recent ascendency of the argument for integrating the income taxes:

> What purported to be a can of rare sardines sold repeatedly, each time at a higher price. When finally an inquisitive purchaser opened the can, he found it to contain worms, not sardines. But why did he open the can?

For years professors enjoyed telling classes in government finance of the evils of an unintegrated income tax and of the beauties of an integrated system. Then policymakers began to take seriously the case for integration, and integration, like the sardines in my apocryphal tale, rose in esteem. But during the last year integration has come under closer scrutiny by those asking whether it would have desirable economic effects and be administratively feasible. It has been judged by some to be desirable and feasible, by others to be a can of worms.

[4] The arguments for and against integration are reviewed in greater detail in Charles E. McLure, Jr., *Policy Options in Integrating the Income Taxes* (Washington, D.C.:

Brookings Institution, forthcoming), chapter 2. The present paper also draws heavily on material in chapters 4 and 5 of that book.

[5] The case for integration is altered but not weakened by the possibility of a shifting of the tax; see McLure, "Integration of the Personal and Corporate Income Taxes," pp. 542-49.

[6] It would, for example, make no sense in an integrated system to apply the limitation on the foreign tax credit at the firm level. But requiring all shareholders who own shares in multinational corporations to complete form 1116 would seem ill advised.

[7] For a discussion of how "integration" means different things to different people, see McLure, *Policy Options*, chapter 2; and Stanley S. Surrey, "Reflections on 'Integration' of Corporate and Individual Income Taxes," *National Tax Journal*, vol. 28 (September 1975), pp. 335-40.

[8] I discuss here only methods that would result in distributed corporate-source income being taxed at the shareholder's personal tax rates. See also McLure, "Integration of the Personal and Corporate Income Taxes," pp. 550-54, for a brief discussion of alternative approaches and their flaws.

[9] One minor difference is that gross dividends would be reported to the shareholder by the corporation, whereas under the imputation method as ordinarily described the firm would report net (cash) dividends.

[10] This traditional view, elaborated more fully in McLure, "Integration of the Personal and Corporate Income Taxes," has recently been challenged in David Bradford, "The Incidence and Effects of a Tax on Corporate Distributions," Center for Operations Research and Econometrics, Catholic University of Louvain, processed, 1977.

[11] Retentions resulting in capital gains realized soon after their accrual could be taxed more heavily than ordinary income, especially if attributable to low-income individuals. For the present discussion, however, this is of limited relevance.

[12] The treatment of tax preferences is discussed in greater detail in McLure, *Policy Options*, chapter 4. The present discussion is entirely in the context of an imputation system both because that is the most likely system to be adopted and because most of the previous analysis has been in that context.

[13] I do not discuss problems that could be overcome if the firm calculated the shareholder's gross-up and credit for him. Examples would include a multiplicity of effective rates, one for each firm, and noncoincidence of the fiscal years of corporations and shareholders. This approach would, of course, entail serious problems of record keeping and communication.

[14] For a further description of the cross-currents that are likely to develop in the debate over integration and dividend relief, see Charles E. McLure, Jr., and Stanley S. Surrey, "Integration of Income Taxes: Issues for Debate," *Harvard Business Review*, vol. 55 (September–October 1977), pp. 169-81.

Summary of Discussion

In commenting on McLure's paper, Attiat Ott suggested that it was vitally important to know who wins and who loses before various forms of corporate tax integration can be evaluated. She noted that the ownership of corporate shares is highly concentrated at the upper end of the income distribution. McLure responded that any reduction in the rate of taxation of corporate capital would raise the rate of return to both corporate and noncorporate capital and that the ownership of the latter is not quite as concentrated as the ownership of the former. Moreover, investors in noncorporate activities might actually experience relatively greater gains in income than owners of corporate securities if the income taxes were integrated, because of the reduction in risk premiums on corporate securities.

Both Martin Bailey and John Nolan believed that there were ways of handling the difficult problems described by McLure and that we should not give up on the idea of integration. McLure replied that his paper was written in just that spirit, but that we should not rush into integration until we had carefully thought through all of the problems that it raises, particularly since he doubted the efficacy of some of the solutions to problems of full integration proposed by Bailey.

With reference to the Boskin-Green paper, Ott and Richard Musgrave stressed the difficulty of determining the "right" rate of capital formation. Boskin replied that his main point was that distortions created by the tax system were definitely leading to too low a rate of saving and investment. James Wetzler expressed doubt that consumption and saving were sensitive to real, after-tax rates of interest, but Boskin stressed that his own evidence indicated a significant, although not a large, degree of sensitivity.

John Berry asked why the savings rate had been so stable through time if it was sensitive to after-tax rates of return. Boskin replied that the net savings rate was more variable than the gross savings rate and that, in any case, there have been many economic and demographic changes that tended to offset each other. For example, there have been changes in the net return, in the age composition of the population, and in the rate of growth of income from period to period.

Richard Musgrave thought that in the short run it would be possible to get a higher rate of capital formation by increasing the rate of resource utilization in a less than fully employed economy, and it was in this spirit that the Carter program was formulated. Boskin suggested that the recovery was well under way, since the unemployment rate had fallen to close to 6 percent, and that it would be increasingly difficult to generate additional capital formation by increasing the rate of resource utilization. On the other hand, Green agreed with Musgrave that there was slack in the economy—particularly in the investment goods sector—and that this may enhance the effectiveness of the investment tax credit. He also noted, however, that it may have more impact on the timing of investment than on its long-run level.

George von Furstenberg said that Boskin and Green had presented a very partial analysis of the Carter proposals in that many indirect policy impacts were ignored. For example, increased grant aid to local governments for things like public service jobs may be used to reduce local taxes, local deficits, or neither, with the effects on aggregate saving and investment depending on the choice made. Furthermore, some types of public purchases may simply provide direct substitutes for private purchases and not impose large resource costs on the economy. Boskin and Green both agreed that these were important issues but stressed the difficulty of estimating their effects. Boskin speculated further that state and localities were more likely to spend additional resources than to reduce taxes.

Richard Musgrave noted that, having accepted an income tax system, we face a conflict between the desire for progressivity and the desire for more capital formation and that the Congress would be unwilling to accept the reduction in progressivity necessary to increase capital formation significantly. More attention should be given to developing measures which would stimulate capital formation while avoiding this conflict. Boskin suggested that attitudes might be changing. We now have an elaborate transfer system devoted to improving the incomes of the lowest part of the distribution, and there is a growing realization that wage earners would be better off in the long run with a higher rate of capital formation. Musgrave responded that wage earners may prefer the short-run benefits of an immediate cut in taxes.